Mrs. Boone's Wild Game Cookbook

Mrs. Boone's
Wild Game Cookbook

Compiled by Judith McGlinn
Illustrations by Edward McGlinn

Momentum Books Ltd.
Troy, Michigan

Compiled by Judith McGlinn
Illustrations by Edward McGlinn

Manufactured in the United States of America
2001 2000   6 5 4 3

Selections and recipes by O.B. Eustis were previously published in *Notes from the North Country* and are reprinted by permission of the University of Michigan Press.
Recipes from several contributors were previously published in *BLM ADO: A Culinary Collection* and are reprinted by permission of Bureau of Land Management, Anchorage District Office.
Recipes submitted by George Burgoyne, Jr. that were previously published in the Michigan Department of Natural Resources pamphlet *Game Recipes* are reprinted by permission of the Department of Natural Resources

Momentum Books, Ltd.
6964 Crooks Road, Suite 1
Troy, Michigan 48098

ISBN: 1-879094-08-8

Library of Congress Catalog Card Number: 92-150320

Preface

Anyone who has been in the same kitchen with a passel of chefs and then tasted their soup will agree that too many cooks spoil the broth. But it's just as true that no one cook could ever live long enough or have the imagination and luck to discover the very best recipes for preparing wild game.

That's why we are so grateful to our contributors and our compiler Judith McGlinn. Judy did a wonderful job gathering these recipes and coddling the copy describing them. To Judy and to our many contributors, and to those clever and resourceful cooks of generations past who handed down these gems—our thanks.

And to our readers, we hope these pages bring as much enjoyment to you as they have to us in producing this volume of our favorite recipes for preparing wild game for the table.

Mrs. B.

CONTENTS

INTRODUCTION

This cookbook is a sampler of favorite recipes from creative and enthusiastic cooks who are comfortable and accomplished in the art of wild game cooking. A constant and recurring theme is consideration for the unique and distinctive qualities of wild game.

If you are "a born cook," you will enjoy using these recipes as a guide or inspiration for culinary experimentation of your own. If you prefer to follow specific ingredients and instructions, you will appreciate the simplicity and clarity of the recipes.

Rabbit, squirrel, beaver, and muskrat take center stage in the first chapter, starring in homey, every day stews as well as exotic gumbos.

Venison is the most popular entrée in this collection, and you will discover a variety of imaginative dishes and a few recognizable favorites as well. The best cuts of venison are the ham (or leg), the ribs, and the shoulder. The distinctive and delicious flavor of young and tender venison is at its best if you don't marinate, overcook, or overseason it.

An appealing variety of game bird recipes, ranging from sautés to barbecues, is offered for both the tentative and the "seasoned" cook. Helpful suggestions and hints assist the cook in determining whether to use a skinned bird or one that is plucked.

From the humble, silvery smelt to the regal salmon, recipes abound for delicate and delectable fish main courses. The selection here is so appetizing, you won't know which recipe to try first.

In Potpourri, you will find interesting and helpful tips as well as an odd assortment of recipes just too good not to include.

Introduction

We are very proud of the selection of recipes in this cookbook, which is a tribute to our fine contributors and those people, sometimes generations back, who passed down these recipes. We call your attention to the list of contributors provided at the back of this book and we gratefully thank everyone who responded so generously.

We especially thank George Burgoyne of the Michigan DNR for permission to use recipes from the DNR booklet *Game Recipes,* and the Anchorage District Office of the Bureau of Land Management in Alaska for permission to publish recipes from *BLM ADO, A Culinary Collection.*

Judith McGlinn
Compiler

GAME PREPARATION

by John H. Williams

One of the truly enjoyable aspects of hunting wild game—bird, fish, or mammal—is to get together afterwards with fellow sportsmen to relive the chase. There is always a camera or two taken along on these outings to help capture the action. Later it's nice to see the pictures and share experiences. Of course, a highlight of the gathering is a shared meal of the bounty.

A victory celebration requires attention and care in the following steps: successful angling or hunting; a good cook and the proper recipe; and just as crucial, the proper care of the animal in the field. Proper care is not difficult, but it is vitally important in order to correctly protect the taste of any captured game. The greatest recipe and the most gifted cook cannot retrieve taste from a tainted piece of flesh. To help ensure your culinary successes later, the time to perform some vitally important preparatory tasks is in the field.

BIRDS

I've hunted geese on many occasions with Cree Indians along the shores of James Bay in the Arctic Circle of Canada. I've always found it interesting the way the Crees protect the meat. They simply split the birds open, from the vent to the sternum, remove all the entrails, and leave everything else intact. They hang the birds so that air movement will circulate around the carcass. At times, we've been out for three, four, or even five days, and the flesh of these birds has never, to my knowledge, shown any ill effect.

If you have access to ice or refrigeration, however, there is another treatment I'd recommend—particularly with smaller, more delicate game birds, or upland birds with their higher fat levels. Whenever possible, gut game birds quickly, following the process mentioned above, and then hang them. (This not only allows for quicker cooling, but also relieves you from carrying the extra weight around.) Depending on the type of bird and the recipe you are likely to follow, skin the bird or pluck it, as soon as it is practical, and then freeze or refrigerate it. If neither of these options is available, ice it down, being very careful to keep the meat itself dry.

Any meat is better fresh, but it's been my experience that all game birds from quail and doves to pheasants and ducks store well in a freezer for at least two to three months. Geese and turkeys freeze well for up to six months.

The hunter should be cautious about hanging all game. If shot up badly, do not hang it. You don't want to encourage the wrong type of bacteria. Hanging mellows and tenderizes the meat if the temperature is cool. It also, however, accentuates the gamey flavor. The factors involved are time, temperature, and your own taste. If the weather is hot, don't hang any game. If you dislike a developed and rather mature taste, stop the hanging when the fat on the game turns a little yellow.

FISH

You've seen those classic photographs of trout fishermen on picturesque streams, fly rod in hand and wicker creel over the shoulder? Beautiful. They conjure up thoughts and feelings as wild as the trout we seek. Well, I wear a creel too—to carry all the extra paraphernalia that I need, but never to carry fish! Rather, I carry a stringer. If I decide to keep a fish, I keep it in the water. In a boat, a live well is great, and so are the wire baskets that float over the side. By all means, attempt to keep your fish alive until you're ready to clean or freeze them.

If you plan on eating fish when fresh, then clean them according to the needs of your recipe. If you're going to store them, I prefer to simply freeze fish whole, innards and all. I believe they last longer that way.

Firm fish, such as perch, walleye, and bluegills freeze well for several months; softer, more delicate fish, such as trout, salmon, and catfish freeze well for only a month or so.

MAMMALS

A friend of mine owns a motel in Crystal Falls in Michigan's Upper Peninsula. Jeri knows that prime hunting and fishing are the main attractions of the area, and she keeps a freezer readily available to her guests. Actually, a lot of motels offer this service, if only you'll ask.

When hunting small game, as with birds, gut them right away, then hang them somewhere to cool. When you have the space, carry an ice chest in your vehicle to ice them down quickly—again, as with birds, being careful to keep the meat dry. Carefully remove all possible fat deposits inside the animal. It's the fat that decomposes most quickly.

With bigger game, such as deer, antelope, bear, and caribou, completely field dress the animal as quickly as possible, always careful to remove the visceral fat deposits, then wipe the cavity clean, and hang it. (Do not wash the cavity unless it's very badly soiled.) Weather dictates how long you can let an animal hang, but I like to allow three to four days if possible—to let the meat cure (tenderize) before processing it.

Game Preparation

None of the precautions and procedures mentioned here are difficult, time consuming or expensive; but they'll all go a long way in ensuring that you, your family, and your friends will fully enjoy the rewards of your hunting and fishing skills.

John Williams, a long-time outdoorsman and a well-known expert on hunting and game animals, especially whitetail deer, is the author of The Deerhunter's Field Guide. *—Mrs. B.*

INTRODUCTION

Fried rabbit is the favorite dish of most rabbit hunters. Rabbit and hare provide excellent entrées and are often used interchangeably with chicken. Rabbit is particularly good when French fried.

George Burgoyne sent me the Michigan Department of Natural Resources pamphlet, *Game Recipes*, which suggests that you should:

> *Substitute rabbit for chicken and if you want to try something out of this world, substitute hare for the chicken in chicken salad. You can't imagine how good it will taste.*

Europeans, most notably the French, consumed prodigious quantities of wild rabbit and hare until these animals acquired a bad reputation as pests. Nonetheless, many excellent recipes, such as Jugged Hare from Belgium and Hasenpfeffer from Germany, have become standards.

Muskrats, like rabbits, are exceptionally prolific, and annually provide fur markets with an abundance of pelts from prime trapping territory in states such as Pennsylvania, Maryland, and Louisiana. Particularly in the south, these critters are commonly known as marsh hares or swamp rabbits, somewhat softening the aversion and queasiness many people may have toward the preparation and subsequent consumption of "rat." Generations of practical rural families confirm that muskrat is surprisingly good eating when properly prepared.

Beavers are capable of attaining a prodigious size—say 50 pounds—and obviously these animals should not be considered for the dinner table, unless you have a very hungry guest. Young beaver weighing approximately eight to ten pounds is a better culinary choice. Be certain to remove musk and castor glands, and all fat. When the recipe requires it, replace the fat with oil, butter or bacon fat.

The Michigan DNR pamphlet gives a good recipe for fried beaver:

> *Use a small beaver cut into pieces. Remove fat and soak overnight in cold water. Drain. Cook in a small amount of water until tender; then fry with bacon and seasoning salt. Try some hickory-smoked seasoning salt on this.*

Moreover, after roasting, searing, and skinning, the beaver's tail becomes quite edible—or so I am told.

O.B. Eustis adopted lower northern Michigan as his home in 1957 and provided several Michigan newspapers, such as *The North Woods Call*, with knowledgeable, interesting, and humorous insights into the natural world with his column called O.B.E.'s Diary. These columns were later compiled in a book titled *Notes From The North Country*. O.B. Eustis died in 1986.

One of my favorite entries from his book is the fond and nostalgic remembrance of deer camp in his native south when he was a boy. Here is his recollection of Hunt Camp Stew:

> *It was a rule in that camp that anyone who got a buck had to quit deer hunting. The lucky hunters were relegated to the pursuit of small game. This supplied a steady stream of rabbits, squirrels, quail, dove, duck, and miscellaneous critters, many of which ended up in the stew pot. Each bowlful was a new adventure in eating.*

> *I remember my uncle telling how to start off one of those stews. Take an old dominicker rooster, four or five old squirrels, a handful of red peppers, some butter beans—and on and on. The recipe is sort of flexible, but for the modern hunt camp stew here's one way to get started. Squirrels should be the basic ingredient.*

Small Game

Disjoint a couple of old squirrels and put them in a pot of water with a couple of venison shanks, or you can use turkey legs if you don't have venison. Add a bay leaf and lots of red pepper flakes. Simmer for a couple of hours until the meat is ready to fall from the bones. Save the stock.

Remove the meat and debone it. This is best done with the fingers, so you can feel the small squirrel bones. Discard the bay leaf. Cover meat with enough of the stock to keep it moist.

In a heavy pot fry out four thick slices of bacon cut in one-inch pieces until they are cooked, but not brown. In the bacon fat saute four or five good hot onions chopped coarsely. Don't brown them. Put the remaining stock, all the meat, and the bacon back in the pot.

Drain a can each of lima beans, whole kernel corn, and tomatoes. Put these in the pot and let it simmer until it's the right consistency. Add a glass of dry vermouth or sherry. Simmer a bit to meld the flavors. Add salt to taste. Serves four. Expand as needed. If you can ever get the hunters out of camp with this stuff on the stove, you'll find it's better the next day. But—I could never wait that long.

SQUIRREL STEW

4 squirrels
2 beef bouillon cubes
2 packages mushrooms
2 cans Irish potatoes
8–10 carrots

$1^1/_2$ stalks celery
2 medium onions
salt and pepper
$^1/_2$ cup dry red wine (optional)

Parboil squirrels until meat falls from bones. Remove meat and chop, taking care to eliminate all small bones. Cool broth and skim fat. Add bouillon cubes, vegetables, spices and meat, and cook until all is tender—and then some. Add wine $^1/_2$ hour before serving.

Carol Bartholomew
Toledo, Ohio

Frost is still in the ground but it has gone from the soul. –Clifford and John's Almanack

FRIED SQUIRREL

squirrel(s)
salt water
flour

$^1/_2$ cup onions
$^1/_2$ cup mushrooms
$^1/_2$ cup cooking oil

Soak squirrel meat in salt water to cover for 1 to 2 hours. Drain well. Cut into pieces and parboil meat for 30 minutes. Roll meat in flour and fry in about $^1/_2$ cup oil. Season with salt and pepper as desired. When meat is about half-done, add $^1/_2$ cup each, mushrooms and onions.

Sandi Douglas
Concord, Michigan

ROAST BEAVER

1 small or medium-sized beaver   **sliced onion**
baking soda   **bacon**

Remove all surface fat. Cover meat with a weak solution of soda and water (1 teaspoon soda to 1 quart water). Boil 10 minutes and drain. Cover beaver with bacon and onions and roast until tender. This will taste like roast goose and will fool anybody. But don't talk about fur coats while eating.

George Burgoyne, Jr.
Michigan DNR

Small Game

BEAVER TAIL SOUP

1 large (or 2 small) beaver tail
1 cup barley
3 onions

3–5 stalks celery
3–5 carrots
seasoning to taste

Scald 2 small beaver tails or 1 large tail so that the outer covering can be removed. Roasting over hot coals gives the same results.

Cut tails into pieces about an inch square, brown in bacon fat and use as the base of stock for the soup.

Add barley, onion, celery, a few carrots and seasoning to your own taste. Simmer slowly for 6 hours.

Jean Krautter
Southwest Wyoming
(sent by Norm Tiffany)

NORTH BRANCH ROAST BEAVER LEG

This is a recipe from my mother's kitchen.

2 beaver hind legs, cut in cubes
salt and pepper
2 sticks butter ($^1/_2$ pound)
2 pounds small onions
1 small can tomato paste (6 ounces)
$^1/_3$ cup red wine
2 tablespoons red wine vinegar

1 tablespoon brown sugar
garlic salt
bay leaf
small cinnamon stick
$^1/_2$ teaspoon whole cloves
2 tablespoons raisins

Remove all fat from meat; season with salt and pepper. Melt butter in dutch oven. Add meat, but do not brown. Arrange onions over meat. Mix tomato paste, wine vinegar, sugar, and garlic salt and pour over meat and onions. Add bay leaf, cinnamon stick, cloves, and raisins. Cover onions with heavy plate to hold them next to beaver. Cover dutch oven and simmer 3 hours on low burner until meat is tender. Do not stir.

Jan Reynolds
Grayling, Michigan

When Jan's mother, Mrs. Johnson, prepared this dish, the aroma wafting from her kitchen would remind you of November days and a crackling wood fire. –Mrs. B.

WILD CRITTER GUMBO

This is a wonderful recipe for using up odds and ends of game. Almost anything tastes good in this gumbo. I've used woodchuck, snowshoe hare, and other small game.

3 cups critter	2 quarts stock
$1/2$ cup flour	1–2 tablespoons cayenne pepper
$1/2$ cup oil (part bacon fat)	1 tablespoon salt, or to taste
1 onion, chopped	$1/2$ cup fresh parsley, chopped
2–3 stalks celery, chopped	$1/2$ cup green onions, chopped

First, you make a roux from the flour and oil. Cook over a low heat, stirring constantly. Traditionalists mandate a cast iron pot. Cook until roux is a rich chocolate color (approximately 30 to 60 minutes).

Add onion and celery. Cook until vegetables are transparent.

Add cold stock. (Adding hot liquid bleaches the roux.) Add cayenne pepper, salt and critter. (Use a combination of texture and fat content, such as half rabbit or squirrel, and half sausage, woodchuck or venison.) Simmer for 1 to $1^1/2$ hours.

Add parsley and green onions 15 minutes before serving. Serve over rice with file powder (ground sassafras).

Julie Loehr
Laingsburg, Michigan

For a milder version of the above recipe, I have a suggestion: Use your cayenne pepper sparingly, say a pinch or two. See how that suits your taste buds. If it's too tame, add a tad at a time 'til you get it to the heat that turns off your thermostat. –Mrs. B.

MUSKRAT SAUTÉ

1 muskrat (1 muskrat feeds 1 person)
lots of water
1 cup of salt
more water
bay leaves
1 large can stewed tomatoes
1 can tomato juice

1 large onion
1 clove garlic
soy sauce
2 ounces Liebfraumilch wine
$1/2$ garlic clove
butter

Prepare muskrat; skin and remove all visible fat. Open up the hind legs along the thighs from the base of tail to knee. Spot the musk sacks and remove.

Add 1 cup of salt to 2–3 gallons of water in large pot. Drop muskrat in and bring to a boil. When water boils, remove muskrat. Put another 2–3 gallons of cold water in pot. Dip muskrat, remove, and rub away excess fat and blood with thumbs. Repeat the process.

Add $1/2$ dozen bay leaves to 2–3 gallons of water. Bring to boil, and add muskrat. When water comes to a second boil, remove the muskrat.

In another pot, put a couple of quarts of water, tomatoes, juice, onion, and garlic. Bring to boil, and add muskrat. Bring to second boil. When legs connected to the skin on the backside crack, the muskrat is done. You can also pinch meat for doneness and tenderness as you would with chicken.

Strain the sauce from the last boiling. Pour some into a pan, heat to the boiling point. Add flour to thicken for gravy. Set aside, keep warm.

Heat sauté pan, add some soy sauce and 2–3 tablespoons butter. Put muskrat in pan, add garlic and Liebfraumilch. Brown the muskrat on both sides. When browned, serve with mashed potatoes and sauerkraut, and gravy.

As an outdoorsman who considers corn flakes and milk a cooking chore, I do not personally have a recipe to provide. Mrs. Anderson, who is an excellent wild game and fish cook, customarily uses recipes from books she has on her shelf, sometimes with personal unwritten modifications.

I have a friend, however, a restaurateur and caterer who specializes in game and exotic offerings. John Kolakowski, of Kola's Kitchen in Wyandotte, provided me with this recipe, which is his favorite way of preparing muskrat. He has let me use it as my contribution. I heartily recommend it.

Tom Anderson
Southgate, Michigan

Tom is a recent and long-time member of the Michigan Natural Resources Commission, a former state legislator, and an ardent conservationist. –Mrs. B.

MICHIGAN MUSKRAT SPECIAL

We use the real name for the animal involved here but you might want to substitute "marsh rabbit" before you put these recipes in your file. People are funny.

1 muskrat (or marsh rabbit, like we said)
1 teaspoon salt
$^1/_8$ teaspoon pepper
$^1/_2$ medium onion, sliced

$^1/_2$ cup fat
1 cup tomato catsup
$^1/_2$ teaspoon Worcestershire sauce

Soak muskrat overnight in salted water (1 tablespoon salt to 1 quart water). Drain, disjoint and cut into desired pieces. Place in deep pan and add 1 quart water, salt, pepper and onion and cook about 1 hour. Melt fat in skillet and fry meat until brown on one side; turn, and immediately pour the catsup and Worcestershire sauce over the meat. Almost cover with water (about 1 cup) and let simmer until gravy is thick enough to serve (about 30 minutes). Serves 4.

George Burgoyne, Jr.
Michigan DNR

MUSKRAT MEAT LOAF

$1^1/_2$ pounds ground muskrat
2 eggs, beaten
$1/_3$ cup dry crumbs
1 cup evaporated milk
$1/_4$ onion, minced or grated

$1/_4$ teaspoon thyme
1 teaspoon salt
$1/_4$ teaspoon pepper
1 teaspoon Worcestershire sauce

Soak muskrat overnight in salted water (1 tablespoon salt to 1 quart water). Remove meat from bones and grind. Mix ground meat thoroughly with other ingredients. Place in meat loaf dish. Place dish in pan containing hot water. Bake in a moderate oven (350°) for $1^1/_4$ to 2 hours.

George Burgoyne, Jr.
Michigan DNR

Come and take pot-luck with me.
My hearth is warm, my friendship's free.
—An Irish Saying

Small Game

RABBIT IN HERB SAUCE

3–4 pounds rabbit, cut up
$1/4$ teaspoon marjoram, powdered
$1/4$ teaspoon thyme, powdered
$1/4$ cup olive oil
$1/2$ cup dry white wine
$1/2$ cup chicken stock
1 teaspoon dried tarragon

3 carrots, thinly sliced
2 medium onions, thinly sliced
1 large bay leaf
2 whole cloves
1 clove garlic, mashed
$1/2$ pound ham, cut in strips

Sprinkle the rabbit with salt, pepper, marjoram and thyme. Heat olive oil and brown rabbit pieces. Add the remaining ingredients and cook covered 45 minutes, turning rabbit several times and adding wine and broth as needed. When ready to serve, warm 2 tablespoons brandy, pour over rabbit and ignite. Serve with parsleyed rice. Serves 6.

Marion Lively
Grayling, Michigan

This is a three-way winner: elegant, festive, and easy. –Mrs. B.

RABBIT STEW

1 rabbit
3 tablespoons butter
1 teaspoon salt
1 cup potatoes (cut like small French fries)
$1/2$ cup celery (cut in strips)
$1/2$ cup carrots (cut in strips)

1 sliced onion
2 cups broth (from the rabbit)
1 cup tomato sauce
$1/2$ cup chopped parsley
$1/4$ cup flour
$1/4$ cup cold water

Cover rabbit with salt water, and stew until tender; drain and save broth. When cold, bone rabbit and cut up meat coarsely. Melt butter in frying pan, add potatoes, celery, onion, and carrots. Cover and cook 15 minutes; then add broth and tomato sauce.

Bring this vegetable mix to a boil and add meat, parsley, and salt. Add thickening and let cook for another 15 minutes. Serves 6 if they're not real hungry. This dish is better than Hasenpfeffer, unless you prefer Hasenpfeffer.

George Burgoyne, Jr.
Michigan DNR

RABBIT IN SOUR CREAM

1 rabbit, cut up
$1/3$ cup flour
$1/2$ teaspoon seasoned salt
$1/2$ teaspoon seasoned pepper

3 tablespoons butter
1 cup sour cream
1 cup half & half

Add seasoned salt and pepper to flour and coat rabbit. Brown in butter. Remove rabbit. Stir remaining flour into pan. Blend in sour cream and half & half. Place rabbit into baking dish and pour the mixture of flour, sour cream, and half & half over rabbit. Bake at 275° for 3 hours.

Mike DeLosh
Auburn Hills, Michigan

To prevent splashing when frying meat, sprinkle a little salt into the pan before putting in the fat. Either that, or have fast reflexes. –Mrs. B.

VENISON

INTRODUCTION

The dictionary says venison is "1: the edible flesh of a wild animal taken by hunting" and "2: the flesh of a deer." We like the first definition because it lets us share with you some great recipes for antelope, elk and moose, as well as deer.

Wild game experts agree on two basic facts: treat venison as you would beef, and compensate for the animal's natural leanness by larding or barding the venison with bacon, salt pork or suet.

Ideally, the hunter was swift and sure in his kill and then field-dressed the game with equal skill. If so, preparation is simple. However, even the choicest cut of venison gets tough and stringy if overcooked. Invest in an accurate timer, and turn over hosting chores to another family member until you, the chef, declare the entrée ready for the table.

In our current national preoccupation with health and fitness, it may be of interest to realize that venison is the healthiest meat we can eat: it is naturally lean and has no chemical additives.

Venison was served with much aplomb on the dining tables of presidents and statesmen in the early American colonies. Perhaps we should continue the tradition.

If you are presented with chops, steaks or roasts that have not received tender loving care before arriving in your kitchen, soak the meat in a savory marinade for 12 to 24 hours before cooking. Some of the gaminess associated with old, hard-run, or improperly dressed venison is masked or changed by the marinade.

The dutch oven and cast iron skillet are basic items of cooking equipment capable of double and even triple duty, moving from stove-top to oven to campfire and camp stove with ease. You'll get many different uses out of your enameled roaster with dome cover, and the electric slow cooker is a handy appliance. In adapting recipes for the slow cooker, liquid ingredients should be reduced by one-third, and herbs and seasonings should be added only during the final cooking stage.

Jayne Koch, a contributor in this chapter, uses venison interchangeably as a substitute for beef; however, she always lards the venison with bacon. Jayne, as well as Mike DeLosch, another contributor, likes to use ground venison in lasagna and Jayne also recommends that $1/3$ ground venison, $1/3$ ground beef, and $1/3$ ground lamb be used to make meat loaf.

Frank Topolewski, a friend from Pinconning who often has hunted antelope in Wyoming, observes: "... if the animal has been run, the odor is quite strong. With the skills I possess as a hunter, my antelope have truly run. The only way I have found to prepare this meat is to cut it into one-inch cubes, roll in flour and fry in butter until brown. It is quite good this way."

Glen Sheppard, the editor and publisher of *The North Woods Call*, submitted a recipe called "Phelps Chops." While he obviously used pork chops in the original recipe, there is every reason why this recipe would work as well for venison chops. Let me give it to you in his words:

A favorite is stuffed chops. Maybe it is a favorite due to the tale that goes with them. Phelps chops were originated by now-retired state forester Jack Lockwood and I during a marathon cribbage showdown. We'd promised to take the girls out, but by mealtime we were still tied. We dashed to the market. The only thing that looked good were these 2-inch thick chops. We sliced them open and started filling them with what was available. The date was January 12, 1974. I still have Jack's check for two bits framed on the wall.

We call them "Phelps Chops" after a ghost town we once owned. They have become one of the favorites of company at our house.

Venison

You start by slicing a pocket in a $1^1/_4$–2-inch thick center cut chop. Into this, sprinkle oregano, nutmeg, dried diced onion and cream cheese. Cook on a charcoal or gas grill, or over wood fire (campfire or fireplace) until done. Do not overdo. Should be juicy when done. Actually, you could stuff them with whatever turns you on.

TIE-ON-YOUR-BIB VENISON ROAST

4-pound piece of venison
salt
pepper

Try to use at least a 4-pound roast since venison shrinks during cooking. Use a rump cut or top of round rolled and tied. Place meat in conventional roasting pan but do not cover or add water. Season with salt and pepper to taste. Roast in low oven, 300° (low temperature retards shrinkage), frequently basting with liquid shortening. Finish basting with juices accumulating from roast. Allow 32 to 35 minutes cooking time for each pound of meat.

Serve venison roast hot because deer fat tends to congeal while it is still warm. If you want to see something funny, serve cold milk or some other cold drink to an uninitiated venison eater.

Serves 1 to 6 people, depending on the people.

George Burgoyne, Jr.
Michigan DNR

Venison

ROAST VENISON TO PLEASE FAMILY

1 venison roast
1 small pork roast
1 package dry onion soup mix

4 whole onions (the more the better)
vegetables of choice

Soak venison roast, with tallow removed, in milk overnight or several hours. Brown both roasts in small amount of shortening. Remove excess fat. Sprinkle 1 package soup mix over the meat. Add onions and 1 cup hot water. Roast at 325° for 3 to 4 hours depending on size of pork roast. Add vegetables of choice during last hour.

Mike DeLosh
Auburn Hills, Michigan

COFFEE POT ROAST

1 package Adolph's Instant Meat Marinade	3–4 pound meat roast
$2/3$ cup strong cold coffee	1 $10^1/2$ ounce can condensed golden
1 garlic clove minced, size to taste	mushroom soup
$1/4$ teaspoon sweet basil	1 large onion, sliced
roux, arrowroot or cornstarch	

Pour contents of instant meat marinade into dutch oven or similar type vessel with tight-fitting lid. Add coffee and blend well; blend in garlic and basil and place meat into the marinade mix. Pierce all surfaces of meat deeply and thoroughly with a fork on both sides. Marinate 45 minutes turning meat a few times. Remove meat. Blend in soup and add onion to marinade; return meat to pan and cook at 325° for $2^1/2$ hours covered. Remove meat from pan, cover with foil, and return to oven to keep warm. Remove all grease from gravy drippings, thicken with roux, arrowroot or cornstarch, and serve over meat and with mashed potatoes. Serves 6.

This is a marvelous recipe for deer, bear, moose, elk, or any red meat roast, including beef chuck roast cut about 2 inches thick. It develops a coffee-chocolate flavor that is great, and it is an easy recipe.

Thomas J. Roney
Grayling, Michigan

Venison

SUNDAY POT ROAST

venison roast
2 cups carrots
potatoes

1 small onion
garlic salt
water

   Put venison in roaster and add enough water to go around, but not over, meat. Add garlic salt to taste and 1 small chopped onion. Roast at 350° about $1^1/_2$ hours; then add carrots and potatoes. Return to oven and continue roasting for an additional hour, or until done.

Sandi Douglas
Concord, Michigan

Don't be fooled by the name—this Sunday Pot Roast is good any day of the week. –Mrs. B.

MILDRED'S VENISON ROAST

4–6 pound roast
$1/3$ cup flour, seasoned with salt and pepper
3 tablespoons bacon fat
1 8-ounce can tomato sauce
1 cup Burgundy wine
$1/2$ cup onion, chopped

$1/2$ cup celery, chopped
$1/4$ cup parsley, chopped
2 carrots, coarsely chopped
1 8-ounce can mushrooms or $1/2$ pound fresh mushrooms
2 tablespoons oregano

Remove all fat and bone from venison; rinse, dry, and dredge in flour mixture. Heat bacon fat in covered roaster or dutch oven. Add meat, brown slowly on all sides. Add other ingredients and bring to boil. Cover and place in 325° oven for 4 hours or until tender, turning roast from time to time. Juices make wonderful gravy!

This recipe is from my mother's kitchen. Mildred Johnson has lived on the North Branch of the Au Sable since her husband took her there on their honeymoon 54 years ago. She is a very special woman, and a great cook. Her recipes have been used for many years in the Johnson household, and I'm sure that you won't be disappointed.

Jan Reynolds
Grayling, Michigan

Venison

PLAIN STEAKS OR CHOPS FOR PLAIN, HUNGRY FOLKS

Cut steak or chops about $^3/_4$–1-inch thick, then treat them exactly like beef steaks.

Or if you want to get a bit fancier …

Rub salt and pepper into steak and dust with flour. Fry in hot fat until brown. Place steak in roaster and cover with mushrooms. Sizzle on top of stove 20 minutes. Remove steak and pour 2 cups of red wine into roasting pan and thicken to make gravy.

For just plain hungry people with meat, potatoes and gravy appetites.

George Burgoyne, Jr.
Michigan DNR

MOM'S ITALIAN BREADED VENISON STEAKS

1–2 venison loins
milk
1 egg, beaten

Progresso Italian Bread Crumbs
olive oil
unsalted butter

Slice venison loins into $1^1/_2$–2-inch fillets. Soak in milk several hours. Remove and dip into beaten egg. Coat with bread crumbs. Lightly sauté on both sides in olive oil and a small amount of unsalted butter. Serve at once. A couple of garlic buds can be sautéed in oil mixture first (and removed before meat is sautéed) for a garlic flavor.

Mike DeLosh
Auburn Hills, Michigan

Venison

SO-O-O GOOD VENISON STEAK

2-pound steak
flour
salt and pepper
1/2 cup vegetable oil

1 cup chopped onion
1 cup chopped celery
1/2 cup chopped green pepper
1 large (28 ounces) can tomatoes

Trim all heavy fat, bone, and gristle from the steak. (Deer, elk or beef can be used.) Place on a floured surface and rub well with garlic salt, pepper and flour. Add more flour and pound thoroughly. Turn and repeat on other side. Cut into serving-size pieces.

In a heavy skillet, heat about 1/2 cup oil. Brown meat well and remove to oiled casserole.

To drippings in skillet, add 1 cup onion, 1 cup celery, and 1/2 cup green pepper (if desired). Stir over medium heat, until tender, scraping up all the "goodies" sticking to the pan. Add tomatoes (cut up). Simmer about 5 minutes, and then pour over meat in casserole.

Bake at 350° for 1 hour.

The first secret: Use well-trimmed meat. If most of the heavy fat is cut off before freezing, it won't have such a strong taste.

Second secret: Beat as much flour as possible into the meat; this makes the meat more tender and helps to thicken the tomato mixture.

This recipe is a favorite of Nina Bitton, my mother, who lives in Pocatello. I grew up eating this, but we called it Spanish Steak with the venison slipped in to replace beef with no one being the wiser. I can remember the shocked expressions on those who enjoyed a lot of meat and then found out afterwards that it was venison.

I know that the "s-o-o good venison" and the "fish log" (see Chapter on Fish) taste good, not just because of my own bias, but because I've watched Mom make lots of people happy over the years, serving these two dishes.

Dennis Bitton
Idaho Falls, Idaho

Dennis is editor of Fly Fishing News *and the quarterly,* The Flyfisher. *–Mrs. B.*

Venison

BAKED VENISON ROUND STEAK

1 round steak	$^1/_2$ cup sliced mushrooms
$^1/_2$ cup sliced onions	1 16-ounce can tomatoes
$^1/_2$ cup chopped green peppers	salt and pepper to taste

Place venison round steak in baking pan and add $^1/_2$ cup sliced onions and $^1/_2$ cup sliced mushrooms over steak. Season with salt and pepper to taste. Add can of tomatoes and $^1/_2$ cup green peppers around steak. Cook $1^1/_2$ to 2 hours until tender at 325–350°

Sandi Douglas
Concord, Michigan

TEXAS MOOSE

moose round steak ($^1/_2$-inch thick)   eggs
salt and pepper   oil
flour

Beat hell out of moose with a Coke bottle, hammer, or fist to tenderize. Poke many holes with fork.

In a paper bag, mix flour and a generous supply of salt and pepper. Dip steak in beaten egg; shake in bag. Repeat process one or more times to get an extra thick coating of flour.

In a large skillet, pour enough oil to fill about $^1/_2$ – $^3/_4$ inch deep. After oil gets hot (about 450° in electric skillet) put steaks in carefully. Cook about 3 to 5 minutes on each side, depending on thickness.

Using drippings, make plenty of cream gravy.

Serve with crowder peas (ask a Texan what these are!), cornbread or biscuits, okra (fried or stewed), and rice. This is a really scrumptious, fattening meal that will make you say an occasional "y'ace" or "y'all." Serve with Cabernet Savignon, Mouton Cadet or any favorite red wine. (If you serve both crowder peas and okra at the same meal, it's best to sleep by yourself for a few nights.)

Cary Brown
Anchorage, Alaska

Cary's recipe for Texas Moose was previously published in A Culinary Collection. *–Mrs. B.*

Venison

MIKE'S STRAIGHT AND SIMPLE CUBE STEAK

venison steaks (to serve 4 to 6)
milk to cover
$^1/_4$ – $^1/_2$ cup flour
2 tablespoons Knorr's Meat Seasoning

bacon fat, oil or shortening for browning
1 package dry onion soup mix
1 large can mushrooms

Remove all tallow from steaks. Soak steaks in milk several hours or overnight. Pat steaks dry and pound with meat mallet or side of saucer to cube and tenderize. Dredge steaks in $^1/_4$ – $^1/_2$ cup flour and 2 tablespoons (more if desirable) Knorr's Meat Seasoning. Coat lightly on each side. Reserve flour. Brown floured and seasoned steaks in bacon fat, oil or shortening of choice, lightly on each side. Remove from pan and add remaining flour, 1 package dry onion soup mix, and 1 large can mushrooms. If gravy is too thick, add some water or white wine. For creamy gravy, use milk. Return meat to pan and simmer until ready to serve.

Mike DeLosh
Auburn Hills, Michigan

VENISON SWISS STEAK

venison steak	**Lipton onion soup mix**
flour	**margarine**

Strip all fat and tissue from steak and remove bones if any. Place between plastic wrap and pound thin. Dip in flour and brown in margarine on both sides. Place in baking dish and add soup mix with water added. Cover with foil and bake at 350° for 1 to $1^1/_2$ hours, depending on amount of meat. Check periodically to see if more water is required.

Cora Miller
Lewiston, Michigan

Venison

OVEN STYLE VENISON CHOPS

venison chops, as many as required   **garlic salt, to taste**
milk to cover chops   **seasoning salt, to taste**

   Soak venison chops in milk overnight in refrigerator. Place drained chops on broiler pan and sprinkle with garlic salt and seasoning salt. Bake in 325° oven for 45 minutes or until done.

Sandi Douglas
Concord, Michigan

VENISON FOR CANDLELIGHT DINING

3 pounds lean venison
2 cups red wine
juice of 1 lime and 2 lemons
2 bay leaves, crushed
2 cloves, bruised
1 clove garlic, mashed

2 stalks celery, chopped
6 slices onion
6 slices carrot
6 peppercorns
1 pinch thyme
$^1/_2$ teaspoon salt

Soak the 3 pounds venison in a brew made from the above ingredients for an hour or so. Then remove and cut meat into 1-inch cubes. Fry in butter until brown. Finally, set meat aflame with 2 tablespoons gin and keep hot.

In another pan, brown 3 tablespoons pork, cubed small. Add this to venison. Strain the marinade mix and pour enough of it over the meat to moisten. If you're still with us, to the meat mix, add 1 cup mushroom buttons, 1 cup small white onions that have been parboiled and tenderized. Cover the whole deal tightly and simmer for 30 minutes.

In another pan, sauté (sauté is fancy for "fry easy") 6 chicken livers and add these to the meat-mushrooms-onion mix. Serve hot, garnished with croutons that have been fried in butter.

George Burgoyne, Jr.
Michigan DNR

VENISON WITH MUSHROOMS

$1/2$ cup thinly sliced mushrooms
2–3 tablespoons onions, finely chopped
2 teaspoons lemon juice
2 teaspoons Worcestershire sauce
$1/4$ teaspoon salt

$1/8$ teaspoon garlic powder
$1/2$ cup margarine or butter
1 pound venison cut in bite-size pieces
rice or noodles

Cook and stir mushrooms, onions, lemon juice, Worcestershire sauce, salt, and garlic powder in $1/2$ cup margarine until mushrooms are tender.

Cook venison pieces in 2 tablespoons margarine until brown and tender. Do not drain. Add mushroom sauce. Stir and cook together about 5 minutes.

Serve over hot cooked rice or noodles.

Susan Aldridge
Winslow, Indiana

VENISON AND BEAN RAGOUT

2 pounds venison in 1^1/$_2$-inch cubes
3 tablespoons oil
1 16-ounce can tomatoes, cut up
1 cup onions, chopped
1 cup dry red wine
^{2}/$_3$ cup water
1 teaspoon sugar
1 clove garlic, minced

^{1}/$_2$ teaspoon salt (optional)
^{1}/$_4$ teaspoon dried thyme, crushed
^{1}/$_8$ teaspoon pepper
1 bay leaf
3 cups potatoes, pared and cubed
1 16-ounce can green beans, drained
1 15-ounce can kidney beans, drained
1 tablespoon cornstarch

Brown venison in hot oil in a dutch oven. Add next 10 ingredients in order. Bring to a boil, reduce heat, and simmer covered 1^1/$_2$ hours. Add potatoes and cook 30 more minutes. Remove bay leaf. Add beans. Combine cornstarch and 2 tablespoons water, and add to stew. Cook and stir until bubbly.

Jayne Koch
Flemington, New Jersey
(sent to us by Jennifer Koch)

I tried this recipe on my family this past year and got a great response. It is very good for venison, and would, of course, work just as well for beef. Mrs. B.

NEW JERSEY STYLE GOULASH

1 medium onion, chopped	2 tablespoons brown sugar
2 pounds venison, cubed	3 tablespoons Worcestershire sauce
3–4 tablespoons oil	$3/4$ teaspoon cider vinegar
$1/4$ teaspoon dry mustard	6 tablespoons catsup
$1^1/4$ teaspoons paprika	2 cups water
$1^1/4$ teaspoons salt (optional)	3 tablespoons flour

Brown venison and onions in heavy fry pan. Combine mustard, paprika, brown sugar, and salt. Combine Worcestershire sauce, vinegar, and catsup and add to mustard mixture. Pour over meat and add $1^1/2$ cups water. Stir, cover, and simmer for 2 to $2^1/2$ hours. Blend flour with $1/2$ cup water. Add to meat mixture and stir until thickened. Serve with noodles.

Jayne Koch
Flemington, New Jersey
(passed on by Jennifer Koch)

VENISON SAUERBRATEN

4–5 pounds venison	**salt and pepper**
2 slices bacon	**3 bay leaves**
2 cups vinegar	**12 cloves**
2 cups water	**2 medium onions, sliced**
$1/_4$ cup sugar	**20 ginger snaps**

Lard venison with small pieces of bacon using sharp knife. Season meat and place in deep bowl. Heat vinegar and water and pour over meat. Add remaining ingredients, except ginger snaps.

Refrigerate for 48 to 72 hours, turning each day.

Remove and place in deep dutch oven. Add 2 cups liquid and blend in ginger snaps. Cook until tender. Add more liquid if needed.

Jayne Koch
Flemington, New Jersey
(Jennifer Koch passed this along)

I'm still wondering why I didn't discover this one sooner—I love ginger snaps used where you'd least expect them. –Mrs. B.

Venison

HOOSIER STEW

1 pound venison, cut in chunks
4–5 potatoes, chunked
2–3 carrots, sliced
1 can cream of mushroom soup

$1/2$–1 teaspoon salt
pepper
$1/2$ cup onion, sliced

Brown meat in 2 tablespoons oil in medium-large pot. Add potatoes, carrots, onion, salt and pepper. Add water to just cover vegetables. Bring to a boil. Reduce heat, cover and cook until vegetables are tender, about 1 hour. Add can of mushroom soup. Stir and cook uncovered about 15 minutes. Serve with hot rolls!

Susan Aldridge
Winslow, Indiana

48

SAVORY STEW

1 1/2 pounds venison, cut in cubes
1 slice bacon, diced
1 small onion, diced
1 carrot, sliced
3–4 fresh mushrooms

3 tablespoons cooking sherry
2 juniper berries
3 bay leaves
6 whole black peppercorns

The peppercorns, bay leaves, and berries are wrapped in cheese-cloth, as in *bouquet garni*. Put bacon in saucepot for a few minutes until limp, add onion, and sauté until transparent. Add venison and brown. Add carrot, celery, and 1/2 cup water and wine. Cover and cook 1 hour. Remove spice bag.

For gravy, mix 2 tablespoons flour with 1/2 cup water. Add to stew and mix well. Let cook for 1 minute. Add 3–4 tablespoons sour cream.

Serve over noodles.

Dorothy Rose
Warren, Michigan

Venison

WOODSMAN'S STEW

$1^1/_2$ pounds venison stew meat or roast
1 cup chopped onion
$1/_4$ teaspoon garlic powder
1 teaspoon salt
$1/_4$ teaspoon pepper
1 tablespoon sugar

1 tablespoon vinegar
$1/_8$ teaspoon nutmeg
$1/_2$ cup water
4 potatoes, quartered
4 carrots, cut in large pieces

Brown stew meat in butter or shortening. Add ingredients. Simmer until tender.

Mike DeLosh
Auburn Hills, Michigan

50

CAMP FAVORITE MEATBALLS

$1/2$ pound ground venison
$1/2$ pound ground lean pork
1 medium onion, grated
1 large egg, slightly beaten
$1^1/2$ teaspoons salt, or to taste
3 tablespoons cooking oil
$1/2$ cup flour

1 cup bread crumbs
1 cup milk
1 medium apple, cored, peeled and grated
$1/4$ teaspoon black pepper
$1^1/2$ cups hot water
2 beef bouillon cubes

Soak bread crumbs in $1/2$ cup milk; add egg, apple and onions, meat and seasonings. Work together with a fork 5 minutes until mixture firms up. Wet hands to shape meatballs. Roll each meatball in flour. Heat oil and brown carefully on all sides. Push meatballs to side, remove excess fat leaving about 3 tablespoons. Mix $1^1/2$ tablespoons of remaining flour in pan. Add hot water and bouillon cubes. Cover and simmer 10 minutes. Stir in remaining milk and simmer 5 minutes more. Serve over noodles or mashed potatoes.

Mike DeLosh
Auburn Hills, Michigan

The grated apple adds a subtle aroma. –Mrs. B.

VENISON AND RICE SUPPER

1 pound ground venison	1 cup rice
$1/2$ cup diced onion	1 can tomato soup
$1/2$ cup diced green pepper	1 cup shredded cheese
salt and pepper to taste	

Cook rice as directed on package. Brown ground venison with onions and green peppers (salt and pepper to taste). Add cooked rice to the browned ground venison. Add can of tomato soup; stir together. Simmer until thoroughly hot. Sprinkle with shredded cheese.

Sandi Douglas
Concord, Michigan

PAPRIKA VENISON STEW

2 small red or green sweet peppers, halved
   and seeded
2 medium onions, chopped (1 cup)
$1^1/_2$ pounds ground venison
$^1/_2$ cup canned beef broth

2 teaspoons Hungarian paprika
$^1/_2$ teaspoon caraway seeds
$^1/_2$ teaspoon leaf marjoram, crumbled
1 16-ounce can tomatoes, drained
salt and pepper

Slice peppers lengthwise into $^1/_4$-inch strips. Sauté onions and peppers in oil in large skillet about 4 minutes or until tender, stirring occasionally. Remove with slotted spoon and reserve. Shape meat into a large patty. Brown on both sides in skillet, breaking up as it browns. Return onions and peppers to skillet. Stir in broth, paprika, caraway and marjoram. Break up tomatoes and stir into mixture. Season with small amount of salt and pepper. Simmer gently until ready to serve.

Mike DeLosh
Auburn Hills, Michigan

VENISON CHILI SUPREME

1 46-ounce can V-8 juice
1 14$^1/_2$-ounce can stewed tomatoes
1 package French's Chili-O Mix
2 pounds venison (browned)
$^1/_3$ Spanish onion, finely chopped
3 celery stalks, finely chopped
$^1/_4$ cup vinegar
1 bay leaf
$^1/_2$ teaspoon oregano
$^1/_2$ teaspoon garlic powder
$^1/_2$ teaspoon onion powder
$^1/_2$ teaspoon paprika

1 beef bouillon cube
$^1/_4$ cup barbecue sauce
$^1/_4$ cup catsup
pinch of basil
pinch of thyme
$^1/_4$ teaspoon black pepper
$^1/_4$ teaspoon cumin powder (only if you like it HOT!)
dash of crushed red pepper (DITTO!)
1 teaspoon chili powder (DOUBLE DITTO!)
3 15-ounce cans dark red kidney beans (drained)

Mix all in a large pot. Simmer for 2 hours. Correct the seasoning. Spill in some beer. Simmer 1 more hour. Serve with your favorite bread and plenty of beer to wash it down.

Ray Gietka
Birmingham, Michigan

Enjoy this with good friends on a cold winter weekend. –Mrs. B.

POOR MOM'S LASAGNA CASSEROLE

8 ounces cooked egg noodles
1 pound ground venison
8 ounces tomato sauce
shredded cheddar cheese

4 or more green onions (with tops for
color), chopped
8 ounces cottage cheese
8 ounces sour cream

Brown ground venison in small amount of oil. Add tomato sauce and onions. Simmer 5 minutes. Add sour cream and cottage cheese. Layer noodles and meat mixture in casserole. Sprinkle top with cheddar cheese. Bake in 350° oven until bubbly and cheese melts on top.

Mike DeLosh
Auburn Hills, Michigan

Top the meal with a mixed green salad and sourdough bread. –Mrs. B.

VENISON WITH MICHIGAN MORELS AND GRAVY

1 pound ground meat
lots of morels
1 teaspoon beef bouillon
1 cup water

2 cans mushroom soup
1 can water
margarine

Brown meat in microwave in a colander (so the fat drains).

Sauté morels in margarine. Add bouillon and 1 cup of water. Simmer 2 to 3 minutes. Add cooked burger and 2 cans mushroom soup with 1 can of water. Stir well, and cook until heated through.

Serve with mashed potatoes, over toast, or with noodles.

Since my husband is a hunter, I've tried several ways of adapting beef recipes to venison. One that I have tried many times to duplicate was a recipe my mother used years ago, called Hamburger Gravy. She made it frequently as it was inexpensive. I have finally been successful using venison with morel mushrooms. (Button mushrooms could be substituted for the morels.)

Cora Miller
Lewiston, Michigan

ITALIAN MEAT LOAF

$1^1/_2$ **pounds ground venison**
3 eggs
3 slices bread, soaked in milk
1 teaspoon oregano
1 teaspoon garlic salt

$^1/_2$ **teaspoon salt**
$^1/_2$ **teaspoon pepper**
1 small onion, chopped
$^1/_2$ **cup chopped green pepper**
$^1/_2$ **cup catsup**

Combine meat and eggs and mix thoroughly. Add bread, seasonings, onion, green pepper and $^1/_4$ cup catsup to above ingredients and mix well. Let stand 15 minutes. Shape into loaf and place in baking pan. Pour remaining catsup over top of meat loaf. Bake at 325° for 1 hour, or until done.

Sandi Douglas
Concord, Michigan

Slide a casserole of scalloped corn into the oven alongside your meat loaf and serve with a Waldorf salad. –Mrs. B.

57

Venison

SOUPER VENISON MEAT LOAF

2 pounds ground venison
1 can golden mushroom soup
1 cup cracker crumbs
1 tablespoon Worcestershire sauce

1 egg
1 small onion, diced
$^1/_4$ cup milk

Mix all ingredients together in large bowl. Put in baking pan and bake at 350° for about $1^1/_4$ hours or until done. Gravy can be made from meat loaf drippings.

Sandi Douglas
Concord, Michigan

STACKED CASSEROLE

1¹/2 pounds ground venison
(and/or other meat)
1 large onion, chopped
3 tablespoons olive oil
1/2 cup sour cream
1 can cream of mushroom soup

1 large can mushrooms
1 can Durkee Fried Onions
1 can Pillsbury Buttermilk Biscuits
1 egg, beaten
1/2 cup sour cream

Brown meat and chopped onion in olive oil. Add and stir together 1/2 cup sour cream, mushroom soup, and 1/2 can Durkee Fried Onions. Pour into casserole. Top with biscuits, with each biscuit cut in half and placed in circle. Top and pour over casserole a mixture of the beaten egg, remaining 1/2 cup sour cream, and reserved 1/2 can Durkee onions. Bake at 350° for 30 minutes.

Mike DeLosh
Auburn Hills, Michigan

Venison

CORNBURGER CASSEROLE

1^1/$_2$ pounds ground meat
2 slightly beaten eggs
1 8-ounce can tomato sauce
^{3}/$_4$ teaspoon salt
dash pepper
1 teaspoon Worcestershire sauce
1 12-ounce can whole kernel corn
^{1}/$_2$ cup medium-coarse cracker crumbs

1 slightly beaten egg
^{1}/$_4$ cup chopped green pepper
^{1}/$_4$ cup chopped onion
2 tablespoons chopped canned pimento
^{1}/$_2$ teaspoon salt
^{1}/$_4$ teaspoon rubbed sage
1 medium tomato, peeled and cut in wedges
^{1}/$_2$ cup sharp American cheese, shredded

Combine meat with 2 beaten eggs, tomato sauce, ^{3}/$_4$ teaspoon salt, pepper, and Worcestershire sauce. Spread half of mixture in an 8x8x2 baking dish. Combine remaining ingredients, except tomato and cheese, and spoon over meat. Cover with remaining meat mixture. Bake at 375° for 1 hour. During the last 5 minutes, arrange tomato on top and sprinkle with cheese. Serves 6.

Mike DeLosh
Auburn Hills, Michigan

Any wild game such as moose or deer venison can be used. Mike tells us he prefers elk. As we've seen from Mike's other recipes, he knows his wild game and he knows how to cook it. –Mrs. B.

CHOWDER, MY WAY

1 cup cooked venison, chopped
$1/4$ cup onions, chopped
1 can mixed vegetables

3 slices bacon, cut in pieces
$1/2$ cup water
1 cup evaporated milk

Cook bacon until crisp. Add $1/4$ cup onions and cook until tender. Stir in vegetables and all liquid. Add venison and cook until hot. Top with parsley. Serves 4.

Sandi Douglas
Concord, Michigan

CREAMED VENISON OVER BISCUITS

1 cup cooked venison
2 cups milk
1 tablespoon butter
$^1/_2$ cup mushrooms

$1^1/_2$ tablespoons flour
$^1/_2$ cup potatoes, diced (optional)
$^1/_2$ cup carrots or $^1/_2$ cup peas (optional)

Cut cooked venison in bite-size pieces and place in saucepan. Add milk with butter. Heat at low temperature. Add mushrooms, potatoes, and carrots or peas, and thicken with flour. Serve over toast or biscuits. Day-old, leftover roast is good for this dish.

Sandi Douglas
Concord, Michigan

STOCKPOT VENISON SOUP

$2^1/_2$ pounds cubed venison
2 quarts cold water
1 cup diced carrots
$1^1/_2$ cups diced potatoes
$^3/_4$ cup diced celery
$^1/_2$ cup finely chopped onion

2 tablespoons finely chopped parsley
3 cups tomato juice
2 tablespoons salt, or to taste
$^1/_4$ teaspoon pepper
$^1/_2$ teaspoon savory
1 tablespoon sugar

Use shank, flank, neck or breast meat. Simmer meat in salted water for 2 to $2^1/_2$ hours, skimming occasionally. Let broth stand in refrigerator overnight or until fat has congealed. Remove congealed fat and add vegetables, juice and seasonings. Simmer slowly for about 2 hours. Mothers: serve this to a hungry family and plan to be adored immediately.

George Burgoyne, Jr.
Michigan DNR

We've tried the Stockpot soup. It's even more delicious the second day, if it lasts that long. We've found that a leaf of lettuce, dropped into the pot, absorbs the grease from the top of the soup. Just remember to remove the lettuce and throw it away as soon as it has served its purpose. –Mrs. B.

Venison

QUICK-AS-A-WHISTLE SOUP

1 pound ground venison
1 cup chopped onion
4 cups water
1 cup diced carrots
1 cup diced potatoes
$1/2$ cup diced celery

2 teaspoons salt
1 teaspoon brown bouquet sauce
$1/4$ teaspoon pepper
1 bay leaf
$1/8$ teaspoon basil
6 tomatoes, or 28 ounces of canned tomatoes (Reduce water to $2^3/4$ cups if using canned tomatoes)

In large saucepan, brown the ground venison; cook and stir onions with meat 5 minutes more or until onions are tender. Stir all remaining ingredients, except tomatoes, with meat and onions; heat to boiling, then reduce heat; cover and simmer about 20 minutes. Add tomatoes; cover and simmer 10 minutes more (until vegetables are tender).

Sandi Douglas
Concord, Michigan

TENDER-SWEET HEART O'DEER

deer hearts
1 cup red wine
2 tablespoons vinegar
1 teaspoon salt

1 small onion, diced
1 teaspoon prepared mustard
2 bay leaves (if you like bay leaves)

If you're too hungry to wait:

Slice deer heart about $3/8$-inch thick crosswise. Fry slowly in butter with onions. A little seasoning salt adds flavor. Fry until tender—cooking it too long makes it rubbery.

If you have time:

Slice deer heart about $3/8$-inch thick crosswise. Mix the above ingredients into a marinade. Marinate (fancy for soak) heart slices for about an hour. Dust in flour and fry 5 minutes in butter.

George Burgoyne, Jr.
Michigan DNR

Venison

DOWN-HOME STIR FRY

$^1/_2$ pound venison
$^1/_2$ cup green peppers, chopped
$^1/_2$ cup onions, chopped
1 cup broccoli, chopped
1 cup tomatoes, chopped
$^1/_2$ cup mushrooms

2 tablespoons shortening
$^1/_2$ teaspoon garlic salt
$^1/_2$ teaspoon salt, or to taste
$^1/_2$ teaspoon seasoning salt
3 tablespoons soy sauce

Cut about $^1/_2$ pound venison in strips and soak in milk for 1 hour. Melt 2 tablespoons shortening in large frying pan. Heat to medium-high. Remove meat strips from milk, drain, and place in frying pan. Stir, and then add peppers, onions, mushrooms, and broccoli. Stir, season with garlic salt, seasoning salt and soy sauce. Stir, add tomatoes and cook 6 more minutes, stirring often. Serve over rice.

Sandi Douglas
Concord, Michigan

BACON-WRAPPED VENISON

venison steak
bacon

Salt and pepper or seasoning salt

Cut steak into serving-size pieces. Sprinkle with salt and pepper or seasoning salt. Wrap each piece with a half or whole strip of bacon. Secure with toothpick. Fry in skillet until done.

Very tasty when grilled on charcoal or gas grill.

Susan Aldridge
Winslow, Indiana

Venison

GOOD-AS-IT-GETS GRILLERS

First prepare a marinade:

$1/2$ cup chopped onion   1 tablespoon Mrs. Dash Original Seasoning
$1/2$ cup lemon juice (ReaLemon for example) $1/8$ teaspoon garlic chips
$1/4$ cup vegetable oil

Combine above and mix well in a glass dish.

Trim away any fat from $1^{1}/_{2}$–2 pounds venison steak and cut into strips about 1-inch wide. Add meat to marinade, cover and refrigerate about 24 hours. Stir or turn occasionally.

Grill over coals about 4 minutes per side depending on desired doneness and temperature of your grill. Don't overcook. Serve hot with sour cream.

A variation: Instead of chopped onion, slice rings from a big Vidalia or Walla Walla onion and grill them after marinating.

This is about as good as it can get.

Jim Gappy
Ann Arbor, Michigan

Jim works with the Michigan DNR Institute for Fisheries Research at Ann Arbor. –Mrs. B.

CHUCK WAGON BARBECUE

1 3–5 pound venison roast (or neck, etc.)
1 large onion, chopped
1 medium green pepper, chopped

1 package dry onion soup mix
1 bottle (18 ounces) barbecue sauce
salt and pepper to taste

Cover meat with water. Cook until tender. Cool. Cut meat into pieces or shred and return to pot. Add other ingredients—onions, green pepper, soup mix, barbecue sauce. Add enough water to cover meat. Simmer until all ingredients are well blended, about 1 hour. Serve on hamburger buns or hot dog buns, or just about any kind of bun you've got.

Can also be done in a slow cooker. More onions, green pepper, or barbecue sauce can be added according to taste.

Charles Baranski
Highland, Michigan

If you carry this dish to a potluck supper once, you're sure to be invited again—and again. –Mrs. B.

THIRTY SECOND VENISON

Everyone should keep something on hand in case friends drop in unexpectedly for dinner. This time of year (winter) we keep venison. We do our own butchering, bone out, and defat most of the meat. For quick resurrection from freezer to table we prefer the loins. We cut out the long strips along the back-bone from the rump to the neck. Professional butchering puts these into roasts or chops. We cut them into convenient lengths and label the packages "loins." Our favorite recipe is called "Thirty second venison."

To thaw, we put the packages in a plastic bag, and submerge in water. In a few minutes it is soft enough to slice. You don't want it thawed completely. Slice the loins across the grain one-fourth inch thick.

While the meat is thawing, mix some blue cheese with your favorite salad dressing to a soft spreadable consistency. We prefer ranch dressing, but mayonnaise is also good. We haven't tried any others.

Spread the meat on aluminum foil. Don't worry if it's still partly frozen. Stick it under the broiler for thirty seconds—NO MORE. Remove and turn it over. Spread the cheese mixture over each venison slice. Return the meat to the broiler for another thirty seconds. Serve immediately or keep on a hot platter until everything is ready. Have the dinner plates warm. Never put venison on a cold dish.

O.B. Eustis

O.B. Eustis lived in Lachine, Michigan. I'm glad we got permission to use this recipe from his book (see credits), it's a winner. –Mrs. B.

INTRODUCTION

Wild fowl, from either woods or water, can be an epicurean delight, a gourmet delicacy, a rare and special treat, and an "adventure in eating." Feathered game also can be an adventure in cooking.

Unlike domestic fowl, game birds possess very little natural fat. Therefore, you will want to add moisture by larding or barding with bacon, salt pork, suet, butter, or olive oil appropriate to the species in hand. Frequent basting is essential, as well, with upland birds such as the milder-tasting pheasant and grouse, which are notably dry.

Thomas J. Roney of Grayling, Michigan, who has sent many recipes our way, says: "... I don't like to skin them if there is any way to avoid it. Game birds are very lean, and what fat may be under the skin is needed for the true flavor, and what fat there is does not compare to a chicken." (*Tom tells me that under ideal circumstances, he picks or plucks the birds while they're still warm. –Mrs. B.*)

A moderate and sensible complement of herbs and seasonings bolsters the natural flavor of wild fowl. A light marinade will especially benefit older waterfowl.

The woodcock, above all other domestic and wild birds, is prized for its firm, wild flavor. O.B. Eustis, naturalist and author of *Notes From The North Country*, has this bit of advice to offer for its proper preparation: "For gourmet woodcock, PICK THE BIRDS. Anyone who skins woodcock can't cook them this way— too dry. Split the birds down the back and marinate in french dressing all day. Broil five or six minutes on each side, starting breast-side down. Baste with the dressing. Don't overcook. Figure two birds per person, and be sure to nibble off the thighs and drumsticks. Try them once this way, and you will never skin another woodcock."

EILEENE'S GOOSE PATÉ

1 roasted goose
    (that turned out too tough to eat)
minced onion, to taste

mayonnaise, to taste
horseradish, to taste
parsley, for garnish

Finely grind cooked goose with meat grinder. Add minced onion, mayo, and horseradish to taste. Mix thoroughly. Shape into ball and garnish with parsley. Use as a spread on crackers.

Eileene Haney
Silver Spring, Maryland

Next time our goose is cooked—too tough or not—we're trying Eileene's goose paté. –Mrs. B.

ALASKAN ROAST DUCK

ducks (1 or more)	**frozen orange juice concentrate**
bacon	**salt**
packaged stuffing mix	**pepper**
apples	

Preheat oven to 350°. Stuff ducks with poultry stuffing (If you don't make your own from scratch, Pepperidge Farms is best!) mixed with chopped apples. Salt and pepper thoroughly. Cover breast completely with bacon strips. Baste occasionally with frozen orange juice concentrate (undiluted). Cook about 45 minutes. Do not overcook; it's best if the meat is still pink. Serve with wild rice, a fresh green salad and a good white wine. This recipe is also good barbecued.

Cary Brown
Anchorage, Alaska

Again we thank the publisher of A Culinary Collection *for letting us use this recipe. –Mrs. B.*

ROAST WILD MALLARD DUCK

ducks	**green peppers**
salt	**tomatoes**
butter	**carrots**
pepper	**celery tops**
onion	

Gently loosen skin around cavity (best done with a long-handled lightweight spoon). Rub salt over breast underneath skin, then force butter mixed with pepper and vegetables (all finely chopped), underneath the skin. Place additional vegetables and seasoning in cavity. Close cavity opening and tie legs together. Place on rack in roasting pan. Roast in 350° preheated oven uncovered.

After 1 hour, pour off fat and add more butter to cavity. Reduce heat to 300° for 2 to 3 hours, depending on number of ducks in roaster. Baste often.

Lulu Harwell
Farmington Hills, Michigan

Lulu Harwell is one-half (Ernie would argue the better half) of the much-beloved domestic team of Lulu and Ernie Harwell. Around Michigan, and points abroad, we have known Lulu's husband as the long-time voice of the Detroit Tigers and a member of the National Baseball Hall of Fame at Cooperstown. Miz Lulu is also renowned from Baltimore to Tacoma for her southern vegetable soup. –Mrs. B.

ROAST DUCK WITH RICE PILAF

Over the years I have used the bounty from our fishing and hunting trips in most of my standard cooking repertoire. A few recipes deserve special mention because they accommodate the unique properties of the game—the flavor and the leanness, for instance.

I hardly ever measure exactly. Most seasoning can be adjusted to taste, and it's fun to experiment. So "an onion" would be a medium onion, or whatever is at hand. A half cup of wine is a reasonable estimate, and there might be a little for the cook, as well.

While duck, pheasant, grouse, etc., are all good in this recipe, I have found it especially good for duck. If the bird has a tendency toward a strong taste, this onion-apple-orange-wine method will dissipate it (maybe I should say mask it—you decide).

birds	**poultry seasoning**
salt and pepper to taste	**1 cup wine**
onions and peeled apples, size and number	**melted butter**
of pieces depends on cavity	**1 or more oranges**
mushrooms	

Grease the bottom of a roasting pan with butter or oil. Sprinkle inside of birds with salt and pepper. Put pieces of onions and peeled apples in birds' cavities. Sprinkle salt, pepper, and poultry seasoning on the outside of the birds. Put birds into pan, pour wine over them, then some melted butter (to combat dryness). Grate the skin of an orange, and reserve. Peel the orange, slice, and put slices in roaster. Roast covered, at 325–350°, until done. Serve the birds with rice, using the following sauce:

Sauté an onion (and mushrooms, if available) in butter. Mix in the reserved orange rind, about 1 tablespoon parsley, and some drippings from the roasted bird. Pour over the rice, and stir.

A note on seasoning. Poultry seasoning can be made out of a number of green herbs—sage, rosemary, tarragon, savory—but I use only two, maybe three, at any one time. Commercial seasoning is also good.

Ruth Favro
Huntington Woods, Michigan

ROAST WILD DUCK (WITH SAUSAGE STUFFING)

2 ducks
1/4 cup finely chopped onion
1/4 cup butter
1/4 cup finely chopped celery
3 cups cubed, day-old bread
1/2 teaspoon poultry seasoning

1/8 teaspoon black pepper
1/4 teaspoon salt
1/2 cup milk
1 egg beaten
1/4 pound pure pork sausage

Add onions and celery to butter which has been melted in saucepan. Cook until transparent and yellow. Add bread and seasoning. Toss to lightly coat with butter. Remove from heat. Add pork sausage. Combine milk and egg and drizzle over bread mixture. Stir lightly to blend. Pack into salted cavities of the birds. Close filled cavities with skewers or toothpicks. Place in roasting pan and brush breast with melted butter or margarine. Place pan in preheated 325° oven. Repeat butter brushing every 10 to 15 minutes for 45 minutes. Cover roasting pan for final hour of cooking. Allow ducks to bake for a total of 1 1/2 to 2 1/2 hours, or until tender. After you've tried this, that duck stamp will seem like a real bargain. Years ago this was a favorite for cooking canvasbacks and redheads. But remember: both are completely protected now.

George Burgoyne, Jr.
Michigan DNR

A-1 ROAST DUCK

Breast of duck, snipe or woodcock is a dark meat which many find a little strong-tasting. Here's the way to make these birds tastier.

several birds, cleaned and ready for the oven   **$^1/_4$ pound margarine**
1 bottle A-1 Steak Sauce   **1 diced apple**

Preheat oven to 350°. Combine ingredients into sauce. Place birds in shallow pan with the sauce, and roast for 40 minutes, basting frequently.

Frank Topolewski
Pinconning, Michigan

CASSEROLE DUCK WITH VEGETABLES

4 ducks (mallards, pintails, etc.)	**¹/₂ cup flour**
1 cup olive oil	**2 cups peas (fresh or frozen)**
12 small white onions	**2 cups dry white wine**
6 large carrots	**4 medium potatoes**
2 cloves garlic	**salt and pepper**

Quarter each duck; rub with salt and pepper. Dust with flour and brown in olive oil in large skillet. Remove from skillet and put aside. In a large casserole with a tight lid, place the onions and carrots (cleaned and cut in quarters, lengthwise), garlic, peas, potatoes (cut in quarters), and salt and pepper to taste. Place quartered ducks on top, add ¹/₂ cup olive oil from the skillet, 2 cups wine, and replace cover. Bake 2 hours at 300°. Goes great with hot biscuits, a big salad, and plenty of your favorite wine.

Cary Brown
Anchorage, Alaska

This recipe from Cary was originally published in A Culinary Collection. *–Mrs. B.*

OLD DUCK, OLD DEER, OLD RABBIT, OLD ANYTHING

meat, old anything
flour
6 onions
1 clove garlic, diced fine
1 pint white wine
$^1/_2$ pint red wine

1 teaspoon salt
spice bag containing
  2 bay leaves
  marjoram
  peppercorns
  parsley

Cut meat into cubes, 1–2 inches. Roll in flour and fry in vegetable oil until brown. Put vegetables and spice bag in pot with wine and salt. Put the browned meat with the wine, vegetables, and spice mix, and simmer 3 to 3$^1/_2$ hours. Remove spice bag and serve meat over rice—preferably wild rice (if you can afford it).

George Burgoyne, Jr.
Michigan DNR

Before you toss out that suspicious roast from way back in the freezer, try this "Old Anything" recipe—bet you'll not regret it. –Mrs. B.

DUCK SOUP

Save the remainder of the drippings from roasted birds. Boil the carcass and take the meat off the bones. Add meat and drippings to the water. Add egg noodles, salt, and pepper; simmer until noodles are *al dente*.

Ruth Favro
Huntington Woods, Michigan

EASY WILD DUCKS IN ORANGE SAUCE

2 wild ducks
2 cloves garlic, sliced
1 large onion, chopped
1 package brown gravy mix
2 tablespoons flour

1 teaspoon garlic salt
1 teaspoon sugar
2 tablespoons plum jam
1 6-ounce can frozen orange juice concentrate, thawed
1 oven cooking bag

Place garlic in duck cavities. Combine and mix well onion, gravy mix, flour, garlic salt, sugar, jam, orange juice concentrate, and 1 cup of hot water in oven cooking bag. Place ducks inside bag and close. Place in roasting pan and slit bag. Bake at 350° for 2 hours. Place ducks on platter and serve with pan juices.

Marcie Raches
West Bloomfield, Michigan

SAUTÉED DUCK BREASTS

This recipe evolved after a one-time try with a borrowed duck press which took two grown men to manipulate and one harried housewife to clean up after.

Carve the breasts from 4 mallards at the time they are shot. This eliminates plucking the birds and also conserves freezer space. Defrost the breasts in a plastic bag saving any juice that accumulates.

8 duck breasts	4 tablespoons chopped parsley
$1/4$ pound butter	1 tablespoon Worcestershire sauce
2 cloves garlic, minced	salt and pepper to taste
Rind of 1 orange, cut in julienne strips and	4 tablespoons currant jelly
poached 2 minutes	7 ounces Marsala

In a large skillet, melt $1/4$ pound butter. Add minced garlic to the butter. When the butter is bubbling, add the duck breasts, and sauté them for 1 minute on each side. Remove the breasts to a warm platter. Add to the butter in the skillet the juices from the defrosted breasts, the poached orange rind, the chopped parsley, the currant jelly, the Worcestershire sauce, salt and pepper to taste, and the Marsala. Blend this mixture well, then return the breasts to the sauce and simmer gently 2 more minutes. The breasts should be pink inside. Serve the breasts with wild rice and any remaining sauce.

Mary Ann Daane
Ann Arbor, Michigan

EASY GRILLED DUCK BREASTS

This is our favorite way to cook duck.

duck breasts, as many as desired
milk, to cover
barbecue sauce, your choice

Soak duck breasts in milk overnight. Remove from milk about 4 hours before cooking; drain, and place into your favorite barbecue sauce. When fire is ready, remove from sauce, and grill, basting frequently with sauce. Cook until pink inside. Serve with extra sauce. CAUTION: Breasts will toughen if over-cooked.

Marcie Raches
West Bloomfield, Michigan

WOODCOCK PATÉ

6–8 woodcock breasts   **8 ounces sour cream**
$1/4$ cup Sherry   **1 package dried onion soup mix**

Boil woodcock breasts for 20 minutes, then mix all ingredients in a blender until desired consistency is achieved. Serve at room temperature with crackers.

Mrs. Don (Cathy) Burkley
Traverse City, Michigan
(sent to us by Thomas C. Hall)

ROAST GAME BIRDS

This recipe is for each small game bird (partridge or game hen). It should be doubled for pheasant.

1 partridge or game hen (skinned)	$^1/_4$ cup dry red wine (Burgundy or Chianti)
$^1/_4$ small apple	$^1/_4$ teaspoon dry parsley
$^1/_4$ small onion	1 pinch each of thyme, rosemary, marjoram
1 slice bacon, minced	$^1/_4$ teaspoon Kitchen Bouquet (to eliminate
1 tablespoon margarine	purple cast due to wine)
1 chicken bouillon cube	salt and pepper to taste
1 cup water	bacon pieces

Stuff game bird with apple and onion. Truss. Fry bacon in heavy skillet. Remove bacon pieces, and save. Melt margarine, add game bird, and brown all over. Remove from pan. Add remaining ingredients to pan drippings. Place bird(s) in covered roasting pan or regular pan which can be tented with aluminum foil. Pour sauce mixture over birds. Cover. Roast at 350° until done (about 1 hour for small birds). When done, remove birds from pan to a hot platter. To gravy in pan, add flour/water mixture (1 tablespoon flour in enough water to form thin paste). Heat on stove, stirring until thickened.

William Stenglein
Grayling, Michigan

BIRD-STUFFED-BIRD
OR BIRD HUNTER'S THANKSGIVING

This recipe keeps both the woodcock and turkey moist and flavorful. It is an excellent combination of light and dark meat. Everyone who has tried it says it is the best woodcock they've ever had. With two German shorthairs, we always have an abundance of woodcock. Many other recipes use only the breast of woodcock. Cooked this way, the legs do not dry out, allowing more of the bird to be used.

1 large wild turkey	1 cup coarse pecans, chopped
4 or 5 whole woodcock	1 loaf whole wheat bread
$^1/_2$ pound sausage	salt
2 cups celery, chopped	pepper
1 cup onion, chopped	sage

Sauté the sausage, celery, onion, and pecans with salt, pepper, and sage to taste. Add bread loaf that has been dampened with water, drained, and torn in small pieces. Rub wild turkey (plucked or skinned) and woodcock with a mixture of salt, pepper, and sage. (A plucked turkey will stay moister.) Stuff woodcock cavities with stuffing, and stuff turkey with stuffed woodcock. Fill any remaining turkey cavity with stuffing. Bake in roaster pan or baking bag for $2^1/_2$ to 3 hours at 325°.

Virginia Pierce and Don Inman
Prudenville, Michigan

PTARMIGAN OF THE PTUNDRA CASSEROLE

3 ptarmigan or sprucehens	$1/2$ teaspoon dried dill weed
$1/2$ cup flour	2 eggs
1 cup bread crumbs, or crushed cornflakes	2 cups sour cream
$1/4$ pound butter (1 stick)	salt
1 clove garlic	pepper

After quartering and drying birds, rub with salt and pepper and flour. Beat eggs with 3 teaspoons water. Roll birds in bread crumbs after dipping in egg, then salt and pepper. Melt butter in large skillet. Split garlic cloves, brown in butter, and remove. Sauté grouse quarters in butter slowly until browned. Remove and place in shallow casserole. Place in preheated oven (350°) and cook for 20 minutes. Add 1 cup sour cream and sprinkle with dill. Replace cover and return to oven for another 20 minutes. Add another cup of sour cream and return to oven for a final 20 minutes. Remove and serve with a gravy, wild rice, fresh corn, and salad. A good white wine really complements this meal. (During certain times of the year sprucehens may be cooked as above and then thrown away. In which case, refer to Cary's Texas Moose recipe in Chapter Two under Venison.)

Cary Brown
Anchorage, Alaska

Thanks again for permission to use this recipe from A Culinary Collection. *–Mrs. B.*

PHEASANT FOR TWO

1 orange	3 cloves garlic (peeled)
1 pheasant	3 sprigs fresh parsley
salt	2 tablespoons butter
pepper	3 slices bacon
$1/2$ teaspoon rubbed sage	1 cup dry white wine
$1/4$ teaspoon paprika	$1/2$ cup golden raisins

Heat wine to boiling in a small saucepan over high heat. Add raisins, remove from heat, and let stand up to 45 minutes.

Preheat oven to 350°. Cut orange in half. Squeeze the juice from half the orange into the cavity and over the skin of the pheasant. Rub the bird inside and outside with the salt, pepper, sage, and paprika. Cut the remaining orange in half and place with the garlic and parsley in the cavity of the pheasant.

Spread butter over the breast and lay bacon crosswise. Place the pheasant in a cooking bag and pour wine-raisin sauce over the top. Bake about 45 minutes.

Using this small amount of butter and adding the cooking bag keeps the pheasant moist.

Carol Hennessy and Ken Nysson
Grand Rapids, Michigan

PHEASANT WITH SHOTGUN SAUCE

2 pheasants
celery
carrots
onions

seasoned salt
pepper
1 cup Burgundy wine

Line roaster with foil. Cut up celery, carrots, and onions. Place pheasants and vegetables in roaster. Season with seasoned salt and pepper. Add 1 cup Burgundy wine, and fold up foil around birds so all moisture will remain inside.

Roast at 300° about $3^1/_2$ hours. Uncover for last $^1/_2$ hour to brown.

Serve birds with the following shotgun sauce poured over them.

Shotgun Sauce:

1 cup currant jelly
1 tablespoon butter
$^1/_2$ teaspoon salt

$^1/_4$ teaspoon garlic salt, or 1 garlic clove
dash of pepper
$^1/_4$ cup Burgundy wine

Combine all ingredients for the sauce in a saucepan; bring to a boil, lower heat, and simmer gently until of desired consistency.

Michele and Rand Oslund
West Bloomfield, Michigan

Rand is a national director of Trout Unlimited; he and Michele know their fish and fowl. –Mrs. B.

PHEASANT IN CREAM SAUCE

1 pheasant, quartered
1 can condensed cream of mushroom soup
$^{1}/_{2}$ cup sour cream

$^{1}/_{2}$ cup, or more, sautéed mushrooms
$^{1}/_{4}$ cup grated Parmesan cheese
$^{1}/_{4}$ cup onion, chopped

Preheat oven to 350°. Rub pheasant quarters with salt and place them in a baking dish with skin side up. Mix together in bowl the mushroom soup, sour cream, mushrooms, cheese, and onion. Spread this mixture over pheasant and bake in oven $1^{1}/_{2}$ to 2 hours or until tender. Serve with oven-baked rice or wild rice. Pheasant can be skinned prior to cooking.

Also, sauce can be doubled if you are cooking more than one pheasant.

Marcie Raches
West Bloomfield, Michigan

PHEASANT 21

This is a real favorite, a never-fail recipe for pheasant, grouse, or even chicken. True wild rice is a marvelous side dish companion. It is said this is much the way pheasant is prepared at New York City's "21" Club.

2 birds, pieced	**1 rib celery**
$1/_8$ teaspoon white pepper	**4 tablespoons butter (not margarine)**
2 bay leaves	**$1/_2$ teaspoon thyme**
$1^1/_2$ cups strong chicken bouillon	**2 tablespoons flour**
1 tablespoon favorite whiskey	**$1/_2$ cup Port wine**
1 large carrot	**1 teaspoon Kitchen Bouquet**
1 onion	

Dice vegetables large and uniformly. Brown birds in butter in dutch oven. Remove. Add vegetables and spices to pan with butter, and brown mixture. Return birds to pan, cover tightly, and cook in preheated oven at 400° for $1/_2$ hour. Remove birds from pan and keep warm. Place dutch oven (pan) on stove burner. Stir flour into juices until brown, then slowly add bouillon, wine, whiskey, and Kitchen Bouquet, stirring constantly to prevent flour from lumping. Boil 5 minutes to desired thickness. Serve over birds and rice generously. Serves up to 4.

Thomas J. Roney
Grayling, Michigan

ONE AND ONLY BAKED PHEASANT

Here is the one and only game recipe I love:

1 pheasant, quartered	$^3/_4$ teaspoon salt
1 can cream of chicken soup	$^1/_3$ cup chopped onion
$^1/_2$ cup apple cider	1 clove garlic, minced
1 tablespoon plus 1 teaspoon Worcestershire sauce	1 can sliced mushrooms, drained
	paprika

Preheat oven to 350°. Place pheasant in ungreased 9x9x2 baking pan. Mix all ingredients and pour over pheasant. Sprinkle generously with paprika. Baste bird occasionally with sauce. Bake uncovered $1^1/_2$ to 2 hours or until fork tender. After baking for 1 hour, sprinkle again with paprika. Simply delicious and deliciously simple!

Louise McGlinn
South Bend, Indiana

Marcie Raches, also a contributor to this chapter, tells us she gets good comments from a recipe much similar to Louise's—a double-good reason to try it. –Mrs. B.

BAKED PHEASANT IN MUSHROOM CREAM SAUCE

4–6 pheasant breasts
bread crumbs
3 tablespoons margarine
$1/2$ pound fresh mushrooms
$1/3$ cup sliced almonds
$1/2$ cup chopped onion
3 celery stalks, chopped

1 pint cream
1 tablespoon salt, or to taste
1 teaspoon pepper, or to taste
dash of garlic
grated Parmesan cheese
1 cup dry Sherry

Dredge pheasants in crumbs and brown in butter; set aside. Sauté mushrooms, almonds, onion, and celery. Place pheasants in dutch oven and cover with sauté. Cover and bake at 350° for $1^{1}/2$ hours. Add cream, salt, pepper and Sherry. Bake an additional 30 minutes. Sprinkle with Parmesan cheese to taste. Bake 5 to 10 minutes and serve.

Serve with wild rice, applesauce, and sautéed carrots.

Thomas A. Baird
Okemos, Michigan

WILD BILL'S PHEASANT RECIPE

4–10 boned pheasant breasts
10 cups apple cider
3 large chunked apples (peeled and cored)
2 onions chunked or sliced
2 teaspoons cinnamon
8 whole peppercorns
2 bay leaves

butter (yes, real butter)
salt and pepper
flour
1 cup heavy cream
arrowroot (cornstarch)
dry white wine (optional)

Place cider, whole peppercorns, bay leaves, apples, onions, and cinnamon in a pot for boiling. Add pheasant breasts, boil until cooked (30–60 minutes), and there is no remaining fat. Melt butter in skillet for browning, being careful not to burn butter. Place flour, salt, and pepper in plastic or paper bag. Wash and dry pheasant and flour lightly. Brown pheasant in butter on all sides until golden (about 6 minutes). Place desired amount of arrowroot or cornstarch in small bowl. Add wine and make thickening. Add cream to skillet and thicken to make sauce. Place browned pheasant in baking dish, and cover with sauce. Bake at 325° for about 15 minutes or until tender. Serve over wild rice with a good dry white wine. Enjoy.

Terry McLoughlin
Toledo, Ohio

OVEN-FRIED PHEASANT

This recipe works for all larger birds, cut into smaller serving pieces, or for whole small birds. It also works for chicken.

2 large (or 6–8 small) birds	**1 teaspoon garlic salt**
2 cups flour	**$^1/_2$ teaspoon cayenne**
1 tablespoon poultry seasoning	**1 box butter-flavored crackers (Keebler**
1 tablespoon paprika	**Townhouse low sodium are my favorite)**
1 teaspoon celery salt	**2 sticks butter or margarine, or other oil**

Turn the crackers into crumbs with a food processor or blender, and put them into a shallow bowl. Melt the butter or margarine, and pour into a shallow bowl. Add the spices to the flour in a brown paper bag.

Dump the pieces or whole birds into the bag and shake until thoroughly coated. Dip into the butter, and roll in the crumbs. Place on cookie sheets or shallow roasting pans and bake at 325° for $1^1/_2$ to 2 hours. Birds will be well done, but the coating prevents them from drying out. Any leftover crumbs can be frozen for future use.

Sandra Eberhart
Alto, Michigan

FRIED PHEASANT

Also can be used for rabbits and squirrels.

2 pheasants
$^1/_4$ pound butter
$^1/_2$ medium-size onion
1 quart milk or cream
2 cups flour

$1^1/_2$ teaspoons salt
1 teaspoon black pepper
2 tablespoons flour and $^1/_4$ cup milk for
    thickening gravy

After birds have been thoroughly cleaned and singed, cut up into pieces as you would a chicken. Dust pieces in flour to which has been added salt and pepper. Brown on both sides in butter. Add the quart of milk or cream and simmer 1 to $1^1/_2$ hours, or until tender. For a cooking variation, add one small can of condensed cream of mushroom soup to the quart of milk or cream.

Remove pieces from frying pan or electric skillet to prepare gravy. Thicken liquid with a batter of 2 tablespoons flour and $^1/_4$ cup milk. Allow to simmer to desired thickness.

George Burgoyne, Jr.
Michigan DNR

BAKED GROUSE WITH AROMATIC STUFFING

2 grouse
1/4 pound butter
6 slices Pepperidge Farm Cinnamon Bread,
    Raisin Bread, or Walnut Bread, crumbled
1 large onion, chopped
1/2 cup walnuts

salt and pepper to taste
1 teaspoon poultry seasoning
1–2 tablespoons flour
brown stock paste
brandy
1–2 cups water

Melt half of the butter and brown the chopped onion and walnuts. Add crumbled bread to mixture. Add poultry seasoning, mix, and season to taste with salt and pepper. Stuff mixture tightly into cavity of birds, letting some stuffing spill over into the bottom of a heavy baking dish. Bake at 350° for 1 hour basting frequently with remainder of the butter. At the end of the hour, the birds should be nicely browned. If not, continue to bake them until they are browned. Pour a liberal dose of brandy over each bird into the baking dish. Remove birds to warm plate. To the butter and brandy in the baking dish, add a tablespoon of brown stock paste. (I use Minors.) Stir the contents, incorporating any bits of stuffing that remain in the pan. Stir in enough flour to make a roux. Heat this mixture stirring constantly. While doing so, gradually add water until the sauce is the desired thickness. Season. Serve grouse accompanied by the sauce.

Mary Ann Daane
Ann Arbor, Michigan

Game Birds

GROUSE AU VIN

Just as good with pheasant or rabbit.

2 birds or 2 rabbits	**1 teaspoon sage**
1 quart Port wine	**2 cups flour**
6 whole cloves	**$^1/_4$ pound margarine or butter**
6 medium sliced onions	**$1^1/_2$ teaspoons salt**
1 large bay leaf	**1 teaspoon black pepper**

After birds have been thoroughly cleaned and singed, cut into pieces as you would a chicken. Combine Port wine, cloves, onions, bay leaf, and sage. Soak pieces in this wine mixture for 2 or 3 days, storing in refrigerator.

Drain the birds, reserving the liquid. Wipe dry and dip in flour to which has been added salt and pepper. Brown on both sides in margarine or butter. Turn the birds and the liquid into a casserole. Cover for baking in a slow oven, 300°, for 1 to $1^1/_2$ hours, or until tender.

George Burgoyne, Jr.
Michigan DNR

BROILED GROUSE

There are about three important rules for cooking grouse: Hang it for several days; don't overcook it; just take the breasts and giblets; the legs aren't worth it.

Romi Perkins in her outstanding book, *Game In Season*, says to draw the bird, hang it in its feathers for 4 to 6 days, at 40° to 50° temperature. My simple rule is to leave it in the refrigerator until ready to cook.

Cooking my own game just adds a facet of interest to my sport. All you have to do is cover the breasts with bacon, and broil for about 15 minutes. A cut into the flesh should show it still slightly pink when ready to serve.

I like to add a challenge: serve the bird with something that is the natural food of the bird, or is found in its environs. Wild rice, flavored with wild grapes and hazelnuts, and applesauce on the side, would be great and natural accompaniments. The giblets can be added to the rice, or saved for paté.

This method is simple, foolproof, and tasty. Enjoy.

Dick Pobst
Ada, Michigan

Dick does more than cook grouse; he's the proprietor of the Orvis Thornapple Shop in Ada, and is the author of Fish the Impossible Places *and the recent* Trout Stream Insects: Orvis Streamside Guide. *–Mrs. B.*

GRILLED BBQ GAME BIRDS

This recipe can be used for *known* young game birds for an outdoor cooking meal. (If birds are older, use Adolph's Unseasoned Meat Tenderizer liberally on birds with salt and pepper.)

Per each bird:

salt and pepper to taste	1 teaspoon onion powder
1 stick margarine ($^1/_4$ pound)	$^1/_4$ teaspoon lime juice
1 teaspoon garlic powder	

Melt margarine in saucepan, stir in garlic and onion powder. Add lime juice, heat well, but do not boil. Cut birds in halves, not pieces. Dust with favorite seasoned salt and pepper to begin, and baste both sides. Briquette fire should be a five count (hold hand over cooking level and count "one Mississippi, two Mississippi, etc., quickly but not fast). Place birds skin side up, baste top with sauce, and cook for $^1/_2$ hour, basting 2 more times. Turn birds, baste again, and cook for 15 minutes or until done. Be very careful your fire is not too hot or the birds will burn badly—although some enjoy the charcoal flavor. Baste well when finished.

Thomas J. Roney
Grayling, Michigan

DORSET RUFFED GROUSE

Begin at 9:00 A.M. on a crisp October morning with two scrambled eggs and one piece of whole wheat toast, buttered. Eggs are to be eaten with Worcestershire sauce. Beverage is a small glass of orange juice.

Kiss wife and/or girl friend goodbye. Be sure to turn on answering machine in study before leaving.

Add one medium-size English setter. Let setter run in the hardwoods behind the house for approximately ten minutes while you enjoy a morning cigarette or pipe. Then instruct dog to kennel up in the back of the truck. Add to the truck a 20-gauge Charles Daly side-by-side, one box of skeet loads, hunting vest, bell for dog.

Drive to favorite grouse cover, arriving exactly at 10:00 A.M. Hunt for six hours with dog. Shoot and kill two ruffed grouse. Only shoot birds the dog has pointed. Field dress and pluck birds on the banks of the nearest trout stream. Leave viscera for the foxes and raccoons. Wash hands in stream.

Drive home, arriving at 4:30 P.M. Kiss wife and/or girlfriend. Check messages on answering machine. Return call to Viking Penguin, instructing them that $20,000 is not enough of an advance on your next book.

Mix a vodka martini: nine parts vodka to one part vermouth. Add lemon twist or olives, as desired.

Clean gun. Feed dog. Tend fire in wood stove. Take shower, preferably with wife and/or girlfriend. Martini can be placed on shelf in shower so that it is not too far away.

Return to kitchen. Preheat oven to 400°. Finish martini.

Game Birds

Slice enough apples to fill cavities of two grouse and place slices inside. Throw in a couple of Concord grapes as well. Bard breasts of birds with several strips of bacon. Place birds in roasting pan.

Cook for approximately twenty minutes, or until flesh is browned on outside, pink in the middle.

Serve whole with spinach salad, baked potato (with butter and sour cream). Serves two and/or three.

Craig Woods
Dorset, Vermont

Craig is the author of The River As Looking Glass *and* The Fly Fisherman's Streamside Handbook—*he has a lucky wife and/or girlfriend. –Mrs. B.*

FISH

INTRODUCTION

The men, women, and children in this country who fish for sport and recreation number in the millions. Because of fishing pressure and environmental constraints, this generation has not enjoyed the unparalleled bounty experienced by our forefathers, and cautionary restrictions have been effected to protect, preserve, and sustain the bounty in our lakes, rivers, and streams. For example, catch and release regulations have been successfully implemented in some heavily fished rivers and even lakes throughout the Great Lakes area and across the United States. In other rivers and lakes, regulations reduce the number of fish which may be legally kept by one individual, more equally distributing the remaining natural wealth.

Angling offers the sportsman a choice of thrills and excitement, relaxation, or aesthetic pleasure, depending upon the individual's pursuit. In addition, the most delicious fish you ever tasted is the one you caught yourself!

Keep your method of preparation simple and uncluttered. Use a light hand on seasonings and go easy on the sauces, always complementing rather than masking the natural flavor of your catch. The result is pure and simple enjoyment.

John Voelker, alias Robert Traver, the author of *Anatomy of a Murder*, *Trout Madness*, and many other wonderful books, sent this short note just before his sudden death in March 1991: "Brook Trout fried with a batch of wild mushrooms added at the end and served along with wild watercress makes me salivate just to scribble it."

His brief comment illustrates just how simple fish recipes can be. Ruth Favro, a contributor to this book, agrees, and offers the following advice:

> "Trout and salmon are good any way you cook them and need little seasoning other than
> salt and fresh-ground pepper, sprinkled on the outside and in the cavity before cooking.

Broil, bake, grill, or fry with or without a coating. Garnish with a wedge of lemon or lime and a sprig of dill or parsley. For all other fish (pike, walleye, bass, etc.,) shake on Old Bay seasoning before cooking."

O.B. Eustis, naturalist and author of *Notes From the North Country*, describes the trapping, preparing and eating of crayfish:

"One of the choicest wild foods in Michigan is probably the least exploited—crayfish—freshwater lobster. They abound, free for the taking, in almost all our lakes and streams.

"Every time I fillet fish, I stick some scraps and backbones in the minnow trap and toss it in the river. Next morning it usually contains two or three dozen crayfish.

"Our river craws average three or four inches long, plus another inch for pinchers. We usually boil them with salt, red pepper, and spices. Five minutes is plenty. We put ours in cold water and turn up the heat. As the water warms, the crayfish relax, go to sleep, and stay nice and tender.

"We like them cold for weekend lunch. Allow plenty of time. Twist off the tail and peel it, then pull off the little dorsal flap, starting at the body end, and discard the mud vein. Pop the choice morsel in your mouth or, if you can wait that long, shuck enough for a cocktail or salad. We also like the claw meat on these river crayfish. A nut cracker is handy for this work, and it leaves plenty of time for leisurely conversation. My New England in-laws say it's just like eating crabs. You can starve to death right at the table. T'ain't so."

NINA'S FISH LOG

2 cups flaked, smoked fish	1 tablespoon horseradish
8 ounces cream cheese, softened	$1/4$ teaspoon salt
2 tablespoons lemon juice	$1/4$ cup finely chopped pecans
2 tablespoons grated onion	2 tablespoons fresh parsley

Combine all but the last two ingredients and mix well. Chill several hours, then shape into a loaf or log. Roll in pecan crumbs, then in parsley. Chill. Serve with assorted crackers. The fish log is something we use every year at the Annual Conclave of the Federation of Fly Fishers. As editor of the organization's magazine, I've held a little open house for several years. Mom (Nina) and Dad have prepared the food and drink for my guests. Dad was a sausage-maker all his life. He's well acquainted with smokehouses and has one of his own now. Getting good smoked fish is crucial to making the recipe work well.

Dennis Bitton
Idaho Falls, Idaho

CARP PATTY CAKES

Raw carp fillets can be ground in a medium-coarse grinder to make nice patties or sausage.

2 pounds ground carp fillets
1 cup soda cracker crumbs
1 teaspoon pepper

2 eggs
$^1/_2$ teaspoon thyme (optional)
1 small onion, diced

Mix fish and ingredients together. Form into patties and fry until crisp, or place in a loaf pan, cover with tomato sauce, and bake at 350° until done.

Ned E. Fogel
Lansing, Michigan

Ned is Manager of the Recreational Fisheries Program of the Michigan Department of Natural Resources. In the July/August, 1984 issue of "Michigan Natural Resources Magazine," his article on Our Most Overlooked Fish *will tell you everything you ever wanted to know about Michigan carp. –Mrs. B.*

CARP SAUSAGE

2 pounds ground carp fillets
$^1/_4$–$^1/_3$ pound ground beef
1 tablespoon Morton's poultry and sausage seasoning

Combine ingredients and mix with masher. Form into patties and refrigerate for 24 hours. Sausage may be frozen. Fry over medium heat 4 to 5 minutes on each side.

Ned E. Fogel
Lansing, Michigan

How about a heaping dish of creamy coleslaw and plenty of cornbread to round out this meal? –Mrs. B.

BAKED CARP WITH PIQUANT SAUCE

2 carp fillets
1^1/$_2$ cups melted butter
3 tablespoons lemon juice

1 teaspoon celery salt
^{1}/$_8$ teaspoon Worcestershire sauce

Put ingredients, except the fillets, in a kettle and heat well. Dry fish fillets and place on flat pan. Brush sauce over fillets, sprinkle with salt and pepper, and bake at 350° for 15 to 20 minutes.

Ned E. Fogel
Lansing, Michigan

Fish

OPEN FIRE WALLEYE FISH FRY

Here's one for walleye that's a bit different. It works best over an open fire. I call it "speed cooking." Four or five hungry campers standing around waiting to eat can have an adverse effect on camp morale.

2 walleye fish fillets	**1 egg**
$^1/_2$ cup Jiffy, Bisquick or pancake mix	**$1^1/_2$ cups club soda or beer**
1 teaspoon Italian seasoning	**some flour**
1 teaspoon poultry seasoning	

Combine all ingredients, except the walleye, for the batter. This batter must be thin. Add milk or more club soda (or beer) until it is the consistency of a thin pancake batter. Roll fillets in flour. Dip in batter, and fry in deep fat or oil until brown at the edges. Flip and cook until done. Serves 4.

Frank Topolewski
Pinconning, Michigan

TWO TROUT FRY

2 trout
2 eggs
$1/3$ cup club soda or beer
1 teaspoon oregano

1 teaspoon poultry seasoning
$1/4$ pound soda crackers
some flour

Reduce crackers to crumbs with blender or rolling pin. Combine eggs, club soda (or beer), oregano, and poultry seasoning into batter. Roll fish in flour. Dip in egg mixture and roll in crackers. Fry in margarine until brown at edges. Turn and cook until done.

A tartar sauce for the fish can be made with 3 tablespoons Miracle Whip Salad Dressing, 1 teaspoon horseradish, or 3 tablespoons catsup with 1 teaspoon horseradish.

Frank Topolewski
Pinconning, Michigan

When grilling whole trout, I like to spray them with Pam non-stick vegetable spray, then sprinkle on my seasonings (Mrs. Dash Lemon, for example). The seasonings stick to the fish, the fish don't stick to the grill, and the skins don't tear open. –Mrs. B.

CHINESE FRIED FISH

1 or 2 large carp (3–5 pounds each)	$1^1/_2$ teaspoons sugar
2 teaspoons Sherry	$^1/_3$ teaspoon ginger powder
1 tablespoon Chinese vinegar	Chinese soy sauce

Scale and viscerate the carp. Cut off all fins (it is better to use scissors, than the knife). Wash the fish.

Slice the fish into pieces obliquely with width about $2^1/_2$ inches. (How oblique depends on the size of the fish: the smaller the fish, the more oblique the cut, so the fish slices do not look too small.) Marinate the slices of fish in soy sauce for about 20 to 30 minutes. (There are two kinds of Chinese soy sauce: the black is preferred.)

Mix Sherry, vinegar, sugar and ginger in a bowl.

Put a wok on the burner to heat. Pour vegetable oil into wok ($^1/_2$ wok level). Put fish slices into oil when oil becomes hot enough. (Do not put more than 2 to 4 pieces of fish at one time.) Turn the fish slices in the oil, using chopsticks, after frying for 2 to 3 minutes. When fish become slightly dark yellow, remove, dip in marinade and serve.

(This recipe was provided by a Chinese scholar, Bin Huang, when he worked with Rick Clark at the Fisheries Institute in Ann Arbor a few years ago. He made a batch for our office and we found it to be quite tasty.)

Jim Gappy
Ann Arbor, Michigan

STEAMED SALMON AND ASPARAGUS

1 teaspoon tarragon
1 teaspoon chives
1 teaspoon chervil
1 tablespoon fresh parsley, chopped

$1^1/_2$ pound salmon fillets, cut into
2-ounce slices
16 medium asparagus spears
$^1/_3$ cup fresh lemon juice
3 tablespoons raspberry vinegar

Combine tarragon, chives, chervil, and parsley in a small bowl and mix well. Add 1 teaspoon of herb mixture to 1 cup of water in a medium bowl and bring water to a boil over high heat.

In a vegetable steamer above the boiling water, place the salmon slices and asparagus. Steam for about 5 minutes or until salmon is flaky. Remove from heat and keep warm.

Combine lemon juice and raspberry vinegar, and pour over the salmon and asparagus which have been arranged on dinner plates. A good complement to this meal is rice or a side dish of boiled redskin potatoes. Garnish plates with lemon wedges and a sprig of parsley and serve.

Ray Geitka
Birmingham, Michigan

GRILLED SALMON AND CORN

salmon steaks or fillets	lemon juice
pat of butter or margarine on each piece	Italian dressing
salt	sliced Spanish onion
pepper	ears of corn
Hungarian (sweet) paprika	

Prepare above ingredients, except for corn, on cookie sheet or in "boat" made of heavy duty aluminum foil with upright sides and twisted corners.

Husk ears of corn. Lay each ear in square of aluminum foil. Wrap ear in foil.

Cook salmon and corn in covered barbecue grill with hot coals. Start corn 5 to 10 minutes before salmon. Grill for 20 minutes more. Turn corn every 5 minutes. Baste salmon while cooking.

Ray Geitka
Birmingham, Michigan

SMOKED SALMON SPREAD

1 pound smoked salmon, flaked
8 ounces whipped cream cheese
5 tablespoons chili sauce

1 teaspoon dill weed
1 teaspoon lemon juice
$^1/_4$ teaspoon onion powder

Mix well. Refrigerate several hours, or overnight, for flavors to mix.

Canned salmon can be substituted if smoked salmon is not available, and I've also found this recipe very good with smoked steelhead.

James D. Schramm
Lansing, Michigan

Jim is the legal counsel for the Federation of Fly Fishers. –Mrs. B.

CUDJOE KEY FISH IN VINAIGRETTE

Michigan Natural Resources Commissioner, Marty Fluharty, put us onto cooking fish in vinaigrette (a vinegar salad oil) during a fishing trip in the lower Florida Keys. It is easy, and one of our many favorite fish recipes.

Unless the fish was caught that day, marinate it for a while in milk. Using a cookie sheet for a base, build a foil pan, with sides an inch, or so, high. Cover the bottom with about $^{1}/_{8}$–$^{1}/_{4}$ inch of vinaigrette. Place the fillets in oil and put on the grill or in the oven. Simmer in oil until fish flakes apart when touched with a fork.

Glen Sheppard
Charlevoix, Michigan

Potatoes hashed in cream and a sunny bowl of carrots with ginger and parsley will nicely complement this well-seasoned fish. –Mrs. B.

SMOKED SALMON PATÉ

$6^1/_2$ ounces smoked canned salmon
$1/_4$ teaspoon Liquid Smoke
1 chopped scallion
4 ounces cream cheese ("lite" is just fine)
paprika

1 tablespoon onion, minced
$1/_4$ teaspoon Greek seasoning
$1/_4$ teaspoon cayenne pepper
parsley sprigs, fresh

Drain canned salmon, reserving 2 tablespoons liquid. Blend salmon and liquid into cream cheese, adding all other ingredients slowly until well blended. Shape into fish form and chill for serving. Garnish with paprika and parsley.

You can also use $1^1/_2$ cups leftover cooked salmon, cut in small pieces and deboned.

Thomas J. Roney
Grayling, Michigan

TROUT AND MORELS SPRING TREAT

small trout	**butter**
morel mushrooms	**heavy cream**
white wine	**flour, seasoned to taste with salt and pepper**

Wash mushrooms, and if you have morels, cut them into rings. If you use other mushrooms, slice them coarsely. (If you can't get morels, oyster mushrooms can be substituted, but it won't be quite the same.) Sauté the mushrooms in a generous amount of butter. When they start to brown, add enough wine to cover them to a depth of about $1/4$ inch. (A good flavorful wine is required; Gewürztraminer is my favorite.) Cook over low heat until almost all the wine has evaporated. Add about twice as much cream as you added wine, and continue to simmer until thick. Salt to taste. As the sauce cooks, dredge the cleaned, whole trout in seasoned flour, making sure that no flour gets inside the fish. When the sauce is done, sauté the fish in butter. You can tell that the fish is ready to be turned over, or removed from the pan, when the inside of the fish is just opaque. This is more of a guide than a recipe. The key ingredients are found, not purchased, and you may never have the same amounts twice. I have tried to note quantities when I made this in the past, and it has never worked. With some skill and common sense, however, a real feast can be had.

Sandra Eberhart
Alto, Michigan

LIME-BUTTER FISH SAUCE

This sauce came from our favorite place in Mexico City. It took five visits on different trips to gain access to the kitchen, and the confidence of the Master Chef, with promises we would not open a restaurant and go into business. It is simple, marvelous and quick, and perfect on oven- or grill-broiled fish of any kind from walleye to halibut. We have used it all over the world on everything.

4 tablespoons salted butter, not margarine
$1^1/_2$ teaspoons lime juice
$^1/_4$ teaspoon Spice Islands Beau Monde Seasoning

Only the above ingredients in these proportions work. Combine all ingredients in a saucepan, and stir over medium heat until butter melts. Do not let butter brown while making sauce. Baste fish well on both sides before broiling, and during grilling, if over a fire. Now, brown remaining sauce and add to fish before serving.

Thomas J. Roney
Grayling, Michigan

PAN-FRIED TROUT

4 fresh trout ($^1/_2$–$^3/_4$ pound each)
juice of one fresh lemon
salt
6 tablespoons flour
$^1/_2$ cup corn oil

$^1/_4$ cup butter
1 slice dry bread, well crumbled
2–3 tablespoons capers
2 lemons sliced
parsley

Wash and pat dry whole trout. Sprinkle with $^1/_2$ of the lemon juice and allow to stand for 5 minutes. Salt trout inside and outside and then roll in flour.

Heat oil in frying pan. Add trout and fry until golden brown (about 5 minutes per side). Carefully remove the trout and discard oil. Melt butter in same frying pan. Place trout back in frying pan and fry for an additional 5 minutes on each side. Remove the trout and arrange on individual plates.

Add bread crumbs to butter and fry until browned. Pour over trout. Sprinkle drained capers over trout, place 4 slices of lemon on each fish, and garnish with parsley. Makes 4 servings.

Serve with pan-fried potatoes and vegetables sautéed in olive oil. Accompany with a chilled white wine and, if available, wild strawberry shortcake for dessert. This recipe is guaranteed to make you the camp gourmet.

John M. Novak
Ypsilanti, Michigan

AMEN! –Mrs. B.

PURE AND SIMPLE WHITEFISH FILLET

whitefish fillet   **flour**
clarified butter   **white wine (Rhine)**

Bring a cast iron pan to medium-high heat. Add butter until it just starts to smoke (a no-no, but it works). Drop fillet into the flour and coat both sides. Place the fillet into the pan flesh side down. Turn once. (Time: 10 minutes per inch.) The last 30 seconds of last turn, add a little wine.

(I once did a Michigan wine and fish demo at Hudson's, and customers did not know what I was cooking. My fish was fresh!)

Len Sokol
Oakland, Michigan

The wonderful cookbook, Culinary Counterpoint, *has this clever tip: Add a piece of fresh ginger to the oil when sautéing fresh fish; it will impart a tangy flavor. –Mrs. B.*

PERE MARQUETTE KING SALMON

3–4 pound salmon fillet, skin removed
$^1/_4$ cup olive oil
1 tablespoon cracked black pepper
1 tablespoon basil
1 tablespoon chopped garlic
1 medium red onion
1 pound fresh mushrooms

1 red pepper
2 fresh lemons
2 cups dry white wine
1 tablespoon parsley
1 tablespoon lemon peel, grated
1 tablespoon orange peel, grated

Preheat oven to 375° and pour a glass of wine for yourself. (You won't use the whole bottle to cook, so ...) Place salmon fillet on a large sheet of foil within a suitable pan. Brush it generously with olive oil and then rub the pepper, basil, and garlic into the fillet lightly.

Chop the onion, mushrooms, and red pepper into medium slices and layer them over the fillet in order. Squeeze 2 lemons over the top of the fish and vegetables, then pour the wine over the entire dish. (Foil should be large enough to contain all liquids.) Sprinkle parsley, lemon and orange peel on top, then cover with an additional sheet of foil. Crimp top foil to bottom foil to form an airtight seal. Bake for 40 to 60 minutes depending on the fillet thickness. Fish should flake, but do not overcook. Cut into serving-size pieces and serve with vegetables on top. Makes 6 servings.

Accompany with a salad of fresh greens and raspberry vinaigrette, wild rice, and Leelanau Wine Cellars Chardonnay.

Fish

This meal is usually served at our cabin on the Au Sable for New Year's Eve. Our neighbors on the river also cook up some great wild game recipes!

Jim Foley
Dublin, Ohio

New Year's Eve, did you say? Set another place. –Mrs. B.

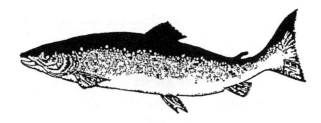

FRESH SMELT (WITHIN ONE HOUR OF THE CATCH)

a mess of smelt
cooking oil
1 frying pan

Real smelt fishermen know the secret of one of the world's finest gourmet meals. After netting a mess of smelt, immediately cut off the heads and gut them. Rinse in cold water and place them in a skillet with $^1/_4$ inch of cooking oil to fry over a camp fire. No breading or batter coating is required. You are simply frying up the fresh natural fish. Turn each one after about 2 minutes and then select one from the center of the pan. Drain it on your plate for 1 minute and taste; if it's crisp, the others will be done, as well. Pick them up, starting at the center of the pan, working outward.

I have enjoyed this royal treat at both the kitchen stove of a cottage and at a fire built right on the beach as we netted the fish.

I can't suggest a cooking temperature, because campfires are hard to control, but keep the frying pan as hot as possible without allowing the cooking oil to smoke.

These morsels are absolutely delicious with a cold beer. The dinner might be high in calories, but it's only a once-a-year experience.

Paul Scupholm
Redford, Michigan

Simple recipes yield tasty treasures. –Mrs. B.

FISH FILLETS WITH ONIONS

orange roughy fillets
mayonnaise
onions, finely chopped
fresh grated Parmesan cheese

fresh ground pepper
salt
paprika

Preheat oven to 375°. Trim fillets to uniform size and thickness. (Save odd pieces for chowder.)

Place on a foil-lined baking pan. Spread each fillet with a thin layer of mayonnaise. Sprinkle finely chopped onion on top. Then sprinkle with fresh-grated Parmesan cheese and season with pepper, salt, and paprika. Bake 10 to 15 minutes or until done.

Lulu Harwell
Farmington Hills, Michigan

Mrs. Harwell advises that this is an easy and delicious way to serve orange roughy, the popular New Zealand fish. We don't know why it wouldn't work just fine for northern pike, bass and other game fish of similar texture. –Mrs. B.

MICHIGAN POACHED SALMON (CHARLEY-STYLE)

2 salmon steaks or fillets
1 tablespoon salt
1 tablespoon white pepper
2 cups water
2 cups dry white wine

$1/2$ cup chopped celery
5 tablespoons chopped parsley, dry or fresh
$1/2$ teaspoon dill weed
1 small pinch tarragon

Mix all ingredients, except fish, in a large skillet, heating until salt is dissolved. Bring this liquid almost to boiling. Place salmon in pan and poach until light pink. Remove fish, saving liquid. Salmon is done at this point. Serve it on a bed of parsleyed rice or parsleyed potatoes.

Use reserved poaching liquid for a very tasty aspic, which is prepared as follows: dissolve 2 packages of gelatin powder in the still hot liquid and chill overnight in a sealed storage container for later use as a cold appetizer, heated for a fish consommé, or as a fish stock for salmon sauces.

Mike Gilder
Warren, Michigan

SOUR CREAM FISH CASSEROLE

2 pounds light or white fish fillets
2 tablespoons butter, margarine, or oil
$1/2$ cup Parmesan or grated cheese
$1/2$ teaspoon paprika

1 cup chopped onion
1 cup sour cream
1 cup mayonnaise or salad dressing
salt to taste

Mix the chopped onion, sour cream, mayonnaise, and salt. Gently melt butter in a large casserole pan. Remove from heat and place fish into pan making sure to coat it thoroughly with the butter. Cover with the sour cream mixture, sprinkle on the Parmesan cheese, and lightly sprinkle paprika over the whole thing. Bake at 350° for 30 minutes.

Mike Gilder
Warren, Michigan

Serve alongside crisp, steamed, mixed vegetables lightly seasoned, and a fresh loaf of Italian or French bread cut in thick slices. –Mrs. B.

CURED AND SMOKED FISH (ROUGH AND LARGE NON-ROUGH)

$1/2$ cup non-iodized salt (kosher)	**$1/4$ teaspoon garlic powder**
$1/2$ cup brown sugar	**$1/4$ teaspoon dill weed**
1 quart water	**2 tablespoons concentrated lemon juice**
1 tablespoon dried chopped onions	**1 medium-large fish (3–5 pounds cleaned)**

Mix all ingredients in saucepan and heat on stove until salt and sugar are completely dissolved. Allow to cool. In a shallow pan, pour brine over fish chunks or fillets, making sure liquid level is above, and completely covers fish. Marinate for at least 12 hours (preferably refrigerated). Remove fish and discard liquid. Pat fish lightly with paper towel and allow to air dry until a glaze forms. Do not rinse. (This will take 1 to 3 hours depending on temperature and humidity.) Fish should then be smoked in your favorite way. (I like to use natural hickory chips; this works especially well on suckers, and may be increased proportionally as needed.)

Mike Gilder
Warren, Michigan

U.P. SALMON CHOWDER

1 pound cooked salmon fillet,
 flaked and deboned
3 tablespoons margarine
1/2 cup chopped celery
2 medium leeks, cut julienne style
1 clove garlic, minced
1/2 cup flour
6 cups water

8 chicken bouillon cubes
1^1/2 cups cubed potatoes
1 cup whole kernel corn
1/3 cup lemon juice
6–8 slices bacon, cooked crisp
 and crumbled
2 cups half & half
white pepper and salt, to taste

Cook celery, leeks and garlic in skillet with margarine until tender but not brown. Stir in flour. Transfer to soup pot and gradually stir in bouillon cubes which have been dissolved in the 6 cups water. Bring to a boil. Add potatoes and reduce heat. Cover and cook for 15 minutes. Stir in fish and lemon juice and cook 15 minutes longer. Add half & half, corn, and bacon. Heat through, but do not boil. Makes 6 to 8 servings.

(We live in the Upper Peninsula of Michigan and often have large catches of salmon. This recipe is the best way to use fillets that are too big for broiling. Our family really loves this chowder.)

Carol Rob
Marquette, Michigan

B-B-Q'D STUFFED FISH

8–10 pound salmon, snapper, or lake trout
salt
pepper
Garden Vegetable Stuffing

$^1/_2$ cup melted butter
$^1/_4$ cup lemon juice
salad oil

Wash fish quickly in cold water and pat dry. Rub cavity with salt and pepper and stuff with **Garden Vegetable Stuffing**. (Recipe follows.) Close opening with skewers and lace with string. Brush fish with salad oil. Place fish in grill basket 4–6 inches from medium coals. Cook 45 minutes or until fish flakes, turning 3 times, and basting with mixture of butter and lemon juice. Serves 10 to 12.

GARDEN VEGETABLE STUFFING

1 cup finely chopped onions
$^1/_4$ cup butter
2 cups dry bread crumbs
1 cup shredded carrots
1 cup cut-up mushrooms
$^1/_2$ cup snipped parsley

$1^1/_2$ tablespoons lemon juice
1 egg
1 clove garlic, minced
2 teaspoons salt
$^1/_4$ teaspoon marjoram leaves
$^1/_4$ teaspoon pepper

Cook and stir onions in butter until tender. Lightly mix in remaining ingredients.

Jan Heimsath
Anchorage, Alaska

Thanks to A Culinary Collection *for letting us use Jan's recipes. –Mrs. B.*

SALMON RICE SQUARES

1 10-ounce package frozen chopped spinach
milk
$^{1}/_{4}$ cup finely minced onion
2 eggs, slightly beaten
1 tablespoon lemon juice
$^{3}/_{4}$ teaspoon salt

16 ounces salmon, cooked, boned, and
   flaked (or 1 15-ounce can, reserve liquid)
3 cups cooked rice
1$^{1}/_{2}$ cups grated sharp Cheddar cheese
3 tablespoons butter or margarine, melted

Cook spinach according to package directions and drain thoroughly. Flake salmon. Add milk to reserved salmon liquid to equal 1 cup. Combine all ingredients. Mix well. Spoon into a greased 8x8x2 baking dish. Bake at 350° 40 minutes or until set. Cut into squares to serve. Makes 6 servings.

Kathie Cruikshank
Anchorage, Alaska

Here's a sure-to-please recipe from the land of the Iditerod, first published in A Culinary Collection. *–Mrs. B.*

WILD BILL'S BARBECUED STEELHEAD

Steelhead fillets
Marinade

Clean steelhead with fresh water. Fish should be deboned with skin left on.

Select marinade from following recipes:

QUICK-AND-DIRTY MARINADE
1 large bottle of Italian salad dressing
1 cup of good dry white wine

BILL'S TRULY BITCHING-OUT-OF-SIGHT MARINADE
1 cube of real butter   **Italian seasonings**
juice of 1 fresh lemon   **salt and pepper**
1 clove of minced garlic (God! How I love   **1 cup of good white wine**
**   the stuff.)**

For this marinade, first melt butter, with Italian seasonings, and garlic added on low heat. Do not allow butter to burn or boil. Add lemon juice and stir. Salt and pepper to taste. Add wine.

Now back to the fish. Place fillets, and most of marinade, in large zip lock bag, reserving enough marinade to baste fish once on the grill. Marinate approximately 4–5 hours. Prepare grill to low even heat. Place fish skin-side up on grill for 3–5 minutes. Turn fish carefully, and baste with remainder of marinade. Close grill cover and cook until skin sticks to grill and fish lifts off the skin. (Fish will poach.)

Serve with:

TERRY'S FISH SAUCE:
   $1/2$ cup Grey Poupon Country Mustard
   $1/2$ cup Miracle Whip
   1 dash Louisiana Hot Sauce (not Tabasco)

Mix thoroughly, and chill $1/2$ hour.

Terry McLoughlin
Toledo, Ohio

INTRODUCTION

Folks who love to cook as much as they love to eat, can't resist bending your ear with stories, experiences, and sure-fire methods and short-cuts.

Our friends have shared some secrets and some tips we'll now share with you. Here are techniques for tenderizing, a process often indispensable to the wild game cook; a touch of sourdough lore and some recipes; easy, fast, and filling foods for ravenous camping companions; condiments that complement game entrées; and a few side dishes to go with any meal.

Sample from these helpful hints, pearls of wisdom, dollops of advice, and snippets of pure nonsense.

BARDING AND LARDING

In cooking wild game, two methods are frequently used to moisten and tenderize the meat. These techniques approximate the "marbling" found in choice and prime cuts of beef roasts and steaks raised for market.

Barding is the process in which you completely cover the meat with strips of salt pork or bacon. (The smokey flavor of bacon may substantially alter the natural flavor of the game; use salt pork when available.)

Larding requires some expertise and a deft hand, but experts agree it's worth the effort. Use a larding needle; fill it with very thin strips of salt pork or bacon, and push it just under the surface and through the meat, going with the grain of the meat. If you do not have a larding needle, you can get a similar effect by inserting thin strips of larding fat with the point of a sharp, thin-bladed knife.

DO-IT-YOURSELF MARINADES

You can't always depend on some old and well-tried techniques, intended for beef, chicken, and so forth, when cooking game. Game is much leaner than domestic meat. Cooking it without added fat can leave it tough and dried out.

We often must rely on marinades, which don't need fat to be delicious. You can create marinades that permeate meat with a lot of flavor.

Marinades should contain at least one acid ingredient, such as fruit juice, vinegar, or wine to tenderize tough meat fibers. Red meats can tolerate lush, sharp blends and should be marinated overnight, or even longer.

Delicate fish, birds, such as woodcock, and even rabbit, require more moderate mixtures; they are also best when marinated for shorter periods. Remember to turn the meat often to expose all surfaces to the marinade.

In the recent past, marinades lacked exotic ingredients. The few bold mixtures had additives like ginger and bay leaves. Now, ethnic spices of all kinds are available with endless possibilities. See if any of the following inspires you to blend your own creation.

For small birds, rabbit or even squirrel:

- non-fat yogurt or skim milk, fresh herbs, minced garlic and hot-pepper sauce.
- either raspberry or sherry vinegar
- orange juice, tomato puree, honey, orange rind, garlic, thyme, black pepper

For venison or larger game:

- orange juice, basil, orange rind, hot-pepper sauce, fennel, coriander, and paprika
- red wine, vinegar, sliced onion, a few peppercorns, and *bouquet garni* of bay leaf, parsley, and thyme
- flavored red vinegar, minced onions, garlic, lemon juice, rosemary, thyme, lemon rind, pepper, parsley and coriander

For fish, try:

- balsamic vinegar, lemon juice, mustard, tahini soy sauce, ginger, garlic, herbs
- white wine, lemon juice, dill weed, chives, and parsley

Potpourri

HUNGRY CAMPER POTATOES AND PASTA

DELUXE BREAKFAST POTATOES

Peel and dice 4 large potatoes. Boil until done. Drain. Cook $^1/_4$ cup onions in 2–3 tablespoons margarine until soft. Turn up heat, add potatoes and brown.

MASHED POTATO CAKES

Mix $^1/_4$ cup onions, leftover potatoes, 1 egg, and 4 tablespoons of flour. Make patties, roll in flour. Fry in margarine or butter until brown.

NIMROD NOODLES

After camping for some time, and eating too much fried food, the body has a craving for high carbohydrates. Noodles and pasta are always a big hit in deer camp.

1 pound dry noodles
1 stick margarine or butter

2 cans of mushroom soup
1 can water packed tuna, optional

Cook noodles according to directions. Drain, add butter, and stir until melted. Add undiluted soup and cook over low heat, stirring constantly until hot for serving. (1 can of water packed tuna, drained, is great in this dish.)

QUICK & HEARTY PASTA

Boil pasta of choice according to package directions. Drain. While still hot, add $^1/_4$ pound margarine and stir until melted. Add some garlic salt and grated Romano cheese to taste. Serve hot.

Frank Topolewski
Pinconning, Michigan

SUPERIOR PANCAKES

Since I have belonged to three different deer hunting clubs, my wife and I were never short of good game recipes. But we also needed a hearty breakfast.

After much competition, it was agreed that there is but one superior pancake recipe. It was passed on to me in 1938 by Grace Bundy (of Bundy Tubing fame). It has passed all tests.

$1^1/_4$ cup flour	$1^1/_2$ cups buttermilk
$^1/_2$ teaspoon baking soda	1 egg
$^1/_2$ teaspoon salt	2 teaspoons shortening
(Add more buttermilk for thinner cakes.)	

While there are many choices for lunch and dinner, one trial will convince the most skeptical. Some may say that a generous shot of Jack Daniels to start improves them. However that is a matter of preference. Enjoy.

George Griffith
Grayling, Michigan

George is one of the founding fathers of Trout Unlimited. –Mrs. B.

CURRIED BROCCOLI AND POTATOES

1 onion
1 tablespoon curry

2 cups broccoli
3 medium potatoes

Sauté a chopped onion in butter and curry powder, say 1 tablespoon. Add broccoli with tender part of the stem, and cut in small pieces. Add small amount of water and stir. Add more curry and stir again, because you probably thought I meant a teaspoon—you must have enough in there. Cover and simmer until the broccoli is barely done. Uncover and reduce liquid to a very small amount. Mix in potatoes that have been peeled, cubed, and boiled. Stir well to coat them with the curry sauce.

I recommend this for serving with fish.

Add tumeric to make the dish more yellow, cumin or red pepper to make it hotter, and coriander to make it more pungent.

Ruth Favro
Huntington Woods, Michigan

NO HOTDOG POTATOES

This dish was devised out of desperation, but has proven to be so good that it has earned a place in my cookbook.

scrubbed, unpeeled potatoes   **aluminum foil**
peeled slices of rutabaga   **a campfire, well burned to coals**
peeled carrots, sliced lengthwise   **(a charcoal barbecue grill will do)**
onion, thinly sliced

Slice the potatoes in half lengthwise, and put one half on a piece of aluminum foil, cut side up. Place a slice of rutabaga, a slice of onion, and several slices of carrot on top of the potato. Put the other half of the potato on top of the carrots (potato sandwich), bring the foil up around the top of the potato to cover, and wrap again with another piece of aluminum foil. Bake in the coals until soft. Serve with whatever you can find as condiments. Catsup works, some people like mustard or mayonnaise, or butter, or just salt.

Sandra Eberhard
Alto, Michigan

TURTLE NUGGETS

Cut the turtle meat into small cubes. Soak meat cubes in salt water for one day (1 tablespoon salt to 1 quart water). Prepare Drake's Batter Mix as directed on package. Drain turtle meat well and dip into milk and Drake's Batter Mix. Fry to golden brown in about $1/4$ inch of oil in frying pan on medium-high heat.

Sandi Douglas
Concord, Michigan
(given to us by Ron Monchak)

Potpourri

ABSOLUTE LOW CALORIE DIET

Note: All meals to be eaten under microscope to avoid oversized portions.

Monday:	Breakfast	diluted skim milk
	Lunch	1 bouillon cube in $^1/_2$ cup diluted water
	Dinner	1 pigeon thigh, fat rendered, 3 ounces prune juice (gargle only).
Tuesday:	Breakfast	scraped crumbs from burnt toast
	Lunch	1 donut hole without sugar
		1 glass dehydrated water
	Dinner	3 grains cornmeal, broiled
Wednesday	Breakfast	boiled-out stains from tablecloth
	Lunch	$^1/_2$ dozen poppy seeds
	Dinner	bee's knees and mosquito knuckles sautéed in vinegar

Thursday	Breakfast	shredded eggshell skins
	Lunch	belly buttons from a naval orange
	Dinner	3 eyes from Irish potato, diced
Friday	Breakfast	2 lobster antennae
	Lunch	1 guppy fin
	Dinner	fillet of soft shell crab claw
Saturday	Breakfast	3 chopped banana seeds
	Lunch	broiled butterfly livers
	Dinner	tossed clover leaf (1) and paprika salad
Sunday	Breakfast	1 defuzzed peach skin
	Lunch	pickled hummingbird tongue
	Dinner	prime rib of tadpole and aroma of empty custard pie pan

Joan Clark
Western Wyoming
(sent to us by Norm Tiffany)

BRINE FOR SMOKING

Here is the brine I use for smoking bear or fish. Use only pickling salt or kosher salt, enough to float an egg in 1 gallon of water. Add 1 cup brown sugar, $1/4$ cup honey, and 2 teaspoons garlic powder. Fish or meat should be soaked for 36 hours at around 45°.

Smoked bear is great!

Frank Topolewski
Pinconning, Michigan

QUICK SUPPER

measure 3 cups flour into a large bowl
answer door
wash 3 cups flour off small son's head
sweep floor
measure 3 cups flour into large bowl, add $1/4$ cup margarine
answer telephone
wipe $1/4$ cup margarine off small son's face and hands
add $1/4$ cup margarine to flour
get crying baby out of crib and rock for 5 minutes
put small son in tub and scrub clean
answer phone
scrape flour and shortening mixture from floor
mix with enough tears to relieve tension
kiss husband as he comes through the door
tell him not to ask
hand him the crying baby
say dinner will be ready in 5 minutes
open 1 can soup
serve with love and remaining strength

Marlene Keeley
Southwest Wyoming
(passed on by Norm Tiffany)

WILD RICE

Wild rice is a natural dish to accompany wild game, especially birds. To each cup of raw rice, add a scant 2 cups of cold water, $1/2$ teaspoon salt, and a dab of butter or margarine to prevent sticking. Stir and cover tightly. Bring to a boil rapidly, stir once and cover again tightly. Turn heat to low and simmer until done, about 14 minutes.

Some notes. A cup of raw rice will serve 2–3 people, depending on how hungry they are. I recall using $1^1/2$ cups of raw rice for 4. Instant rice is not to be considered. The original recipe stated 1 teaspoon salt, but over the years I have decreased it. Leftover drippings from roasted birds may replace a part of the water for the rice to increase flavor.

Ruth Favro
Huntington Woods, Michigan

HARVEST TOMATOES AND STUFFING

$^1/_3$ cup butter or margarine
$^1/_2$–1 teaspoon salt
1 teaspoon basil
$^1/_4$ teaspoon pepper
$^1/_2$ cup diagonally sliced celery
$^1/_2$ cup green pepper strips

$^1/_4$ cup chopped onion
1 cup seasoned stuffing mix
4 medium to large tomatoes,
   cut in 8 wedges each
2 teaspoons sugar, if desired

In heavy 10-inch skillet melt butter or margarine; add seasonings. Sauté celery, green pepper, and onion uncovered over medium heat until tender but not limp. Add stuffing; toss. Add tomatoes and sugar and toss gently. Cover; continue cooking until tomatoes are hot through, yet firm (10 to 12 minutes). Makes 4 servings.

Vi Grady
Farmington Hills, Michigan

This side dish will likely steal the show from your entrée—it's that good. Serve it with anything from burgers to poultry. Make plenty to accommodate requests for second helpings. –Mrs. B.

PEACH HONEY

12 large peaches
2 small oranges
sugar

Peel peaches and remove pits. Grind peaches on coarse setting. Grind oranges with peel on. Combine and measure. Add equal amount of sugar. Boil about 25 minutes until thickened. Pour into jars and seal. Jam thickens, so let stand about a month before using.

Norm Tiffany
Thayne, Wyoming

He who flatters the cook never goes hungry. —Old Proverb

DANDELION JELLY

1 quart blossoms
1 quart hot water
1 package pectin

2 tablespoons lemon juice
4$^1/_2$ cups sugar

Gather well-developed blossoms without stems early in the morning when dandelions are still closed. Wash well; clip and discard green parts. Pour hot water over blossoms. Boil 3 minutes (if longer it will turn green!). Strain through cloth. This will be about 3 cups of juice. Add pectin, lemon juice, and sugar. Boil 3 minutes. Jar and seal.

Norm Tiffany
Thayne, Wyoming

PEACH CHUTNEY

3 cups white vinegar	6 medium apples (McIntosh)
8 cups sugar	1 large Bermuda onion
1 teaspoon ginger	4 sweet red bell peppers
1 teaspoon allspice	1 cup white raisins
$1/2$ teaspoon ground cloves	1 cup currants
$3^{1}/_{2}$ pounds peaches	

Boil vinegar, sugar, and spices for 15 minutes. Peel and chop the peaches and apples. Add to syrup and cook 10 minutes. Grate onion and chop peppers. Add to syrup and cook 35 minutes more. Stir often. Add raisins and currants and cook additional 5 minutes. Put in sterilized glasses and remove air bubbles with a knife. Seal at once. Try adding a little curry if desired. Especially good with game. Yield: 8 pints.

Marcie Raches
West Bloomfield, Michigan

Great house gift. –Mrs. B.

156

PRUNE CATSUP

1 quart ground prunes (Italian prune plums)	1 teaspoon mustard
4 cups sugar	1 teaspoon cinnamon
$1/2$ to 1 quart vinegar	1 teaspoon salt
1 teaspoon cloves	3 medium onions, ground fine
1 teaspoon pepper	

Boil ingredients 1 hour, stirring frequently to prevent scorching. Bottle while hot. This is a great sauce for pork roast or game meat.

Shari Hollinger
Anchorage, Alaska

Shari's recipe first appeared in A Culinary Collection. *–Mrs. B.*

INDIA RELISH

1 peck (12$^1/_2$ pounds) medium-green tomatoes $^1/_2$ cup salt
3 medium onions   6 cups distilled white vinegar
1$^1/_2$ cups celery $^1/_2$ cup yellow mustard seed
4 medium sweet red peppers   5 cups sugar
2 medium green peppers

    Clean vegetables. Remove stem end from tomatoes, skins from onions, tops from celery, and seeds and cores from peppers. Put all vegetables through the coarse grind of a food grinder. Add salt and allow to drain for 1 hour. Heat vinegar, mustard seed, and sugar to boiling. Add vegetables and boil gently for 10 minutes, stirring occasionally. Carefully pour boiling mixture into hot, sterilized jars, filling to $^1/_4$ inch from top. Be sure vinegar solution covers all vegetables. Seal each jar immediately after it is filled. Yields 8 pints.

Vi Grady
Farmington Hills, Michigan

This recipe is from the kitchen of Mrs. Katherine Scheuer, an Ohio farm wife and mother of thirteen children, who began her married life at the turn of the century in a home she and her husband built together. The relish is prepared and enjoyed in the homes of several granddaughters and great-granddaughters. –Mrs. B.

A SOURDOUGH YARN

Various stories tell of the sourdough starter's origin. Here's one of the more credible "tall tales".

"Sourdough Pete", when a young man, came to Alaska from Michigan at the turn of the century to seek his fortune. His grandmother, who had pioneered in the Michigan woods, knew a thing or two about the hardships in a new land. Her parting gift, a crock of yeast starter for hotcakes and bread, made him famous over the land. With the help of a sack of flour, "Sourdough Pete" always had hotcakes to eat whether he struck it rich or not. He shared it with friends who, the story tells, walked miles to renew or get a starter of the yeast product. Pete became known for his generosity and his name, "Sourdough Pete", originated.

Thanks to A Culinary Collection *for "Sourdough Pete's" story, as well as the following recipe for Sourdough Sponge. –Mrs. B.*

SOURDOUGH SPONGE

Place the starter in a medium-size mixing bowl. Add 2 cups warm water and 2 cups flour. Beat well and set in a warm place, free from draft, to develop overnight. In the morning, the batter will have gained $^1/_2$ again its bulk and be covered with bubbles. Set aside $^1/_2$ cup sponge in the refrigerator jar for your sourdough starter for next time.

Rye bread will do you good,
Barley bread will do you no harm,
Wheaten bread will sweeten your blood,
Oaten bread will strengthen your arm.
                    An Irish Proverb

SOURDOUGH QUARTET

Here are four delicious sourdough recipes from Charlene Montague of Anchorage, Alaska. –Mrs. B.

SOURDOUGH BREAD

2 cups sourdough sponge
4 cups sifted flour
2 tablespoons sugar

1 teaspoon salt
2 tablespoons fat
$^1/_4$ teaspoon soda added later

Set sponge as above and let stand in warm place overnight or for 6 to 8 hours. Save $^1/_2$ cup for next starter. The remaining sponge should be about 2 cups.

Sift dry ingredients into a bowl, making a well in the center. Add fat to the sponge and mix well. Pour into the well of flour. Add enough flour to make a soft dough for kneading. Knead on a floured board for 10 to 15 minutes. Place in a greased bowl. Cover with a towel and let rise in a warm place for 2 to 4 hours or until doubled. Dissolve the $^1/_4$ teaspoon soda in a tablespoon of warm water and add to the dough. Knead it in thoroughly. Shape dough into loaves in bread pans and set aside to rise. When doubled, bake at 375° for 50 to 60 minutes.

SOURDOUGH WHEAT BREAD

2 cups sourdough starter sponge   **2 tablespoons sugar**
1 cup whole wheat flour or graham flour   **1 cup white flour**
1$^1/_2$ teaspoons salt

Combine ingredients and mix well with flour—this sponge will be sticky. Set on a warm well-floured board. Knead 1 or more cups white flour into the dough for 5 to 10 minutes. Shape into a rounded loaf and place in a well-greased pie pan. Grease sides and top of loaf, cover with a towel and let rise 1 hour or until doubled.

Bake in preheated oven at 450° for 10 minutes, then reduce heat to 375° and bake 30 to 40 minutes longer. Makes one large loaf.

If starter is very sour, add $^1/_4$ teaspoon soda to the flour that is kneaded in on the board. –Mrs. B.

SOURDOUGH HOTCAKES

2 cups sourdough sponge   **1 teaspoon salt**
1 or 2 eggs   **1 tablespoon sugar**
1 teaspoon soda

Add ingredients to sponge. Beat with a fork and blend in all ingredients. Add 2 tablespoons melted fat. Bake on a hot griddle. Turn once. Yield: servings for 3 people.

For interesting variations, add $^1/_2$ cup whole wheat flour; cornmeal; wheat germ; or bran flakes to the batter. (2 eggs will provide the liquid for this addition.) –Mrs. B.

SOURDOUGH MUFFINS

2 cups sourdough sponge
$1^1/_2$ cup whole wheat flour
$^1/_2$ cup sugar
1 teaspoon salt
$^1/_4$ cup dry milk (non-fat)

1 teaspoon soda
1 cup raisins (optional)
$^1/_2$ cup melted fat
1 or 2 eggs

Sift dry ingredients into a bowl. Make a well in the center. Mix egg and fat thoroughly with the sponge. Add this to the well in the flour. Stir only enough to moisten the flour. Fill greased muffin tins $^3/_4$ full. Bake in 375° oven for 30 to 35 minutes. Yield: 20 small or 12 large muffins.

If a cracked dish is boiled for 45 minutes or so in sweet milk, at the end of that time you'll find that the crack will be so welded together it will hardly be visible, and the dish will be so strong it will stand the same usage as before. –Mrs. B.

Potpourri

FRETLESS FRITTERS FOR WILD GAME BREAKFAST

1 batch of George Griffith's "Superior Pancakes" (page 144) or 1 package buttermilk pancake mix
1 pint, whole kernel sweet corn

1 pitcher genuine maple or wild berry syrup
Enough of your favorite sausage, patties, or small steaks of wild game
Creamery butter or the nearest thing to it

Timing and technique are as important as the ingredients in this simple recipe invented by a pilgrim who had seen one too many bowls of oatmeal and never heard of cholesterol.

Preparations start the next time you have a batch of great sweet corn. After cooking, slice off the rows just near enough to the cob that you get all the good stuff and none of the bad. Get small bags of this into the freezer right now to lock in the sweetness.

Time passes.

It is now a winter morning when your breath freezes and the ice on the pond heaves up like rifle shots. In a separate skillet, cook up your favorite wild game meat patties, sausages or small steaks. Time it so the meat will be at its crackling best just when your fritters are finished. If you're up to it, fix your eggs over easy so later you can dip forkfuls of your fritters into the warm, gooey yolk.

When your large skillet or grill is hot enough to make a few drops of water jitterbug a couple seconds before evaporating, pour or spread cooking oil, then ladle or pour the runny batter in puddles twice the size of silver dollars. The mixture has to be thin, otherwise you'll end up with more of a corn pancake which is edible but not in the same league as a fritter. As soon as you've got four or five of these spitting at you, grab up a good handful of corn kernels and sift them onto and into the cooking fritters. They'll nestle right in and get steam cooked just right in the next minute or two. Keep a close eye on that first fritter, peeking at its bottom as you lift it with a spatula. As soon as it's past golden but short of burned, start flipping. You'll get a different sound as the second side hits the griddle and the corn starts to sear.

Be ready with the meat and eggs that you've been cooking over to the side; stack them on the left half of pre-warmed plates, turn out the fritters onto the open half and deliver crackling hot. At the table, top with butter and maple syrup or strained wild berry syrup. Make twice what you think you'll need.

Bill Haney
Bloomfield Hills, Michigan

You truly don't have to wait for breakfast. Try these fretless fritters instead of potatoes, yams, or wild rice beside a dinner venison roast or wild fowl main dish. –Mrs. B.

ALPHABETICAL LIST OF CONTRIBUTORS